II

# No Problem is Permanent

How empowering great people can help you overcome any challenge

# Lloyd Ansermoz

Copyright © 2025 Lloyd Ansermoz
All rights reserved
ISBN: 9798291652589

To Naomi for all your love and belief in everything we do together, and to our amazing children and grandchildren for their unconditional love and unwavering inspiration.

Thank you also to my <u>real</u> friends in life and business, you know who you are.

To the wonderful Sue Evans – a dear friend, confidant and wizard with numbers.

To my Obi-Wan Kenobi – Laurence Udell - you made me be different and I am forever grateful.

To Mom and Dad for creating me and to my three sisters and brother for being there with me growing up and still loving me.

# Table of Contents

| | |
|---|---|
| Author's note | XV |
| Introduction – Adversity is just a hurdle…. | XVII |
| Chapter 1 – Enterprising beginnings… | 1 |
| Chapter 2 – Ambition on loan… | 10 |
| Chapter 3 – Chasing validation… | 25 |
| Chapter 4 – Growing through flaws… | 38 |
| Chapter 5 – Success is never a solo act… | 53 |
| Chapter 6 – Shifting barriers… | 65 |
| Chapter 7 – Still an outsider… | 79 |
| Chapter 8 – The end of the beginning… | 91 |
| Chapter 9 – A blessing in disguise… | 106 |
| Chapter 10 – It's just what we do around here… | 124 |
| Chapter 11 – Full circle… | 145 |
| Chapter 12 – Life always gives you another turn… | 158 |

# Chapter Topics

## Contents

### Introduction - Adversity is just a hurdle

Adversity in life is inevitable. How you overcome adversity is up to you. For me, overcoming adversity required a huge amount of self-development and learning. This journey also inspired my commitment to creating inspiring team cultures.

### Chapter 1 - Enterprising beginnings

When you're a kid, you don't really understand what being short financially means. Everyone around you is in the same boat. Then, when you get into secondary school, it hits you. My motivation both in school and in my early career was to earn as much money as I could, as soon as I could.

## Chapter 2 - Ambition on loan

Working in a massive dairy gives me my first experience of business relationship building. Deals were being done, growth was everywhere, but somehow, I wasn't feeling valued. It seemed that validation was even harder to get than an annual bonus.

## Chapter 3 - Chasing validation

Some first steps into franchising, a deal I wished I hadn't made, and after months of tireless work, some bargaining power, came my way. Then a phone call completely out of the blue changes my life forever. A new role leaves the validation that I'd spent so long searching for within touching distance.

## Chapter 4 - Growing through flaws

Sometimes you make decisions that you regret later in life when you're trying to get ahead. Everyone is flawed in some way and an essential part of growth involves reflecting on those flaws and trying to do better business in future. This reflection left me with a massive decision: to stay with one business or to go out and launch my own.

## Chapter 5 - Success isn't a solo act

You can't do it on your own! Entrepreneurs become successful because great people share their vision and join them for the journey. If you try to do everything completely on your own then you won't achieve anywhere near the success that you would enjoy alongside a talented team. This involves changing the way you think. Very often, obstacles within your own mind can stop you from taking great advice and embracing even better partnerships.

## Chapter 6 - Shifting barriers

Awards dinners, huge contracts and more growth than I ever could have imagined wrap themselves up in the whirlwind of success that follows my first business, *Keen Kleen*, making its mark. A career that had started with cleaning cellars takes me to a wonderful lunch with one of the world's most famous billionaires and his top team. Things seem like they can't get any better.

## Chapter 7 - Still an outsider

As *Keen Kleen* expands into a new sector, I feel lonelier than ever before. Success brings pressures that entrepreneurs rarely talk about and often suffer through in silence. Keeping everything together is tougher than I ever could have imagined.

## Chapter 8 - The end of the beginning

Fighting to save *Keen Kleen* took almost everything out of me and the business. Putting the pieces of my life back together wouldn't have been possible without the support of wonderful people like Naomi. A Californian course gives me a new purpose and gives my life a new meaning.

## Chapter 9 - A blessing in disguise

Cancer. It's the word nobody wants to hear. My life is turned upside down as I'm diagnosed with a brain tumour and only given 2 weeks to live. Somehow, I survive the operation. After that, my faith comes back and powers me on to new successes both personally and professionally.

## Chapter 10 - It's just what we do around here...

Cancer comes back but that won't stop my team and I building another business. This business is different though. *Fidelis* incorporates three decades of learning on team culture to build a

Happiness-Centred Business. While much of the industry focuses on selling to clients, we refer to them as 'partners' and collaborate with them to sustain mutual long-term happiness and growth.

## Chapter 11 - Full circle

*Fidelis* grows from strength to strength. There's no tragedy this time. The perfect broker gets in touch and our Happiness-Centred Business sells on excellent terms. A new opportunity allows me to help entrepreneurs to build happiness in their own businesses.

## Chapter 12 - Life always gives you another turn

An opportunity to give business coaching sessions to prisoners allows me to help people who have taken a wrong turn in life as they find the right one. Our prisons are bursting with skilled people. Those people just need some help using their skills in ways that benefit themselves and society. After one of these sessions, I look back on my career with a colleague. Even in the darkest of moments, faith can lead you to remarkable successes. I reflect on why I'd not known that when I was younge

# Authors Note

This book has been a long time coming, mainly because I have had so much going on that it has needed updating every week for the past 40 years!

I have been an avid reader for many years. My love of reading began after some of the most inspirational people I've had the pleasure of meeting inducted me into the business world all those years ago. To this day, I am so grateful to them for taking me to new levels of understanding about both how the corporate business world works, and more importantly, how that same world affects our personal lives at every level for good and sometimes not so good. Books have inspired me so much that making this book even a little inspirational for you would be another goal ticked off my list.

My life in business has had its ups and downs and inevitably, so has my personal life. Both constantly get intertwined. Understanding how they can both work together to bring harmony and success all round has required me to learn how to make decisions proactively and tackle difficult situations head on. Learning how to work on and invest in myself through my own personal development and finding the right people to be around has changed my life at all levels. It's been a journey of overall joy but hasn't been without its major challenges. My learning journey isn't over yet either!

We can all make a difference in our lives if we want and need to. Many of us are already happy with our lives and what we are doing. That's fine, but there are plenty of us out there who (deep down) would really like to make meaningful changes in our lives.

## No Problem is Permanent

Sadly, we often just find it too difficult to get started because of the influences around us. Maybe it's a lack time; the restraint of a job; a lack of money; relationships at home; or hanging out with the wrong groups. Whatever these influences are, there's always a way to move forwards in life. Change is inevitable in all our lives in one form or another.

Taking massive action to bring massive change really is possible for everybody. There are going to be people around you who will not understand why you are making those changes and there are people who may even be hurt by the changes that you are going to make. Don't let that put you off taking action to change your life for the better though!

Ultimately, if you have a plan to create your own journey and destination in life for the good of yourself and the most important people around you, then that's taking action and it's OK.

I met Tom O'Brien at events several times before speaking with him about being able to help me in writing my book. I had been concerned about writing a "warts and all" book about me, but at the same time, I was inspired about how I might be able to help others. Tom has guided and advised me and put up with me throughout this journey and I am ever thankful to him for driving me forwards to achieve yet another goal in my life. Thanks Tom.

I'd also like to thank the wonderful team at *Lamwyk* for publishing my book, and my friends at *Levells* for their awesome cover design.

# Introduction

## Adversity is just a hurdle

You never forget some phone calls. I was sitting at my desk when the Facilities Manager of one of the UK's biggest engineering companies rang. Normally they were delighted with our cleaning services - but not that day.

"After yesterday's Board meeting, my colleagues saw your CLEANERS putting food into boxes and taking it home!" said the furious voice on the other end of the line, only just avoiding shouting.

At *Fidelis*, we always avoided using the word 'cleaners'. Cleaning requires immense skill. If you're meeting clients in a dirty room, then you won't sell anything apart from apologies. We always referred to our colleagues as 'cleaning operatives' or 'cleaning technicians' to give them the respect that their skills and talents deserved. This particular client didn't share our view. After a Board meeting where lots of perfectly good food hadn't been eaten, their first reaction when some of our operatives tried to stop it going to waste was to jump to a false conclusion and accuse them of stealing. The client had assumed that all 'cleaners' were somehow dodgy or shifty and that they had no right to take away what was deemed uneaten company property.

Stripping people of their humanity and judging them based on assumptions in a moment of anger is an awful thing to do, yet so many of us do it so often without thinking. If something happens that you don't like, don't just jump to conclusions (we've all done it at some point unfortunately). Instead, consider why it happened that way and how you could introduce new systems and processes to get a different outcome. Let people prove themselves to you too. Never let your assumptions of how people might behave cloud your judgement of their actual behaviour.

# Culture eats strategy for breakfast…

Many business owners might react suddenly without allowing proper time for reflection after receiving a call like that from a client. The obvious choice on the table seemed to be between compromising our values and disciplining our cleaning operatives or walking away from a large contract. I saw things differently.

After arranging to meet the client in-person as soon as possible, I suggested, "Why don't we bring in a policy to say that our cleaning operatives should put any uneaten food they find straight in the bin?"

The Facilities Manager then replied, "Well…no don't do that. I…suppose… it's OK if they box leftover food up after they've finished working."

From then on, they began to see our cleaning operatives as people who were just doing the right thing in preventing food waste. They never complained about the practice again and continued working with us for many years. Changing approaches to company culture in the businesses we serviced was a fundamental part of what we did at *Fidelis* (founded in 2011). Our own company culture centred around making sure that businesses across the country saw cleaning as a profession and not just a job. This outlook ensured that clients properly valued and respected our cleaning operatives. It gave our business greater value too. When we sold the company for a £multi-million return in April 2021, that culture added at least a further quarter percentage to our final sale price. 'Culture' isn't just another buzzword. Getting culture right means that you can offer your customers and your teams more, all while boosting your profits. The *Fidelis* brand was

Introduction

derived from our core values of trust, honesty and professional excellence. Those values sat at the heart of the culture that we were building for the business. The name '*Fidelis*' literally translates as Faithful, Honest and Loyal Friend in Latin. Loyalty and honesty sat at the heart of the exquisite service that each of our clients received. That's why every single member of our Fidelis team received customer service training as standard procedure. As a result, they were naturally courteous and helpful to anybody they met or spoke to in the buildings we serviced. This enabled us to generate a higher pay rate for our professionally trained operatives, resulting in a higher charge rate and therefore a higher profit margin for our business. We then invested those profits to maintain industry-leading levels of customer service in an era of immense technological and social change. Our aim was always to be world-class across every area of our business. These performance levels were non-negotiable.

This approach marked a significant personal change from the beginning of my business career. In those early days of my working life, I was always driven solely by boosting my own income to my own benefit. The prospect of a nice new car featured much more in my thinking than social responsibility or boosting other people's wages. That determination to buy everything I'd ever wanted led me to travel around the UK to spend days on end stripping asbestos out of cellars in commercial buildings across the country. The work was highly hazardous but paid well (the extra cash went a very long way in the 80's). Many of my friends were earning a lot less at that time.

A talent for finding a commercial advantage, earning good money, and developing new business skills and acumen pushed me through the ranks at various facilities management (also known as FM) companies. FM is usually split into two categories: Hard and Soft. Hard FM focuses on maintaining physical aspects of a building's infrastructure such as lifts, and the systems that the building can't function without such as heating, lighting and plumbing. Soft FM covers everything else and mainly focuses on creating clean and safe spaces for people to live and work in. It became clear to me that a lot of these companies operated through clunky, outdated processes that would hugely limit the quality of their Hard and Soft services (and therefore their revenues) as we approached the year 2000. Money came first in almost all of my decisions back then. It was my passion for pushing the envelope in search of profitability that led to co-founding *Keen Kleen*

(2000-2007) which proudly serviced national rail providers and other large corporate firms.

So what moved my priorities away from money? Life.

## Overcoming adversity...

A very traumatic divorce just as *Keen Kleen* was hitting the peak of its success forced me to re-evaluate what mattered in life. The material wealth that I had built up over the years began to disappear as the strain of the divorce on the business became significant and we lost key contracts. Adversity is only a setback if you see it that way though. A sunny day in California in 2006 changed my life forever by teaching me to view each moment of adversity as a hurdle to overcome rather than a crushing failure. That trip to California showed me how to free myself from the grief, fears and frustrations behind my purely self-motivated approach and start shaping my own destiny. The £ half-million court order that I was required to pay my then ex-wife after filing for divorce on returning to the UK was just another hurdle. Almost everything went. She even claimed the personalised number plate on my car. However, these losses were nothing I couldn't come back from.

So many business owners struggle with divorce. A part of you disappears and before you have time to fully process what's happened, you're inundated with legal papers and all sorts of costs. These awful moments are actually the perfect moments to shape your own future and take control of your life. You can't change what's happened, but you can determine the person you'll become. Two battles with Cancer within six years brought more adversity than I ever thought I'd have to deal with. However, they also brought my faith back. Faith undoubtedly gave me the strength to overcome hurdles that I didn't have the physical energy to jump over.

Faith can represent religious belief and certainly did in my case. However, faith takes other forms too. It's also faith in people: trusting in their better nature and desire to do the right thing. Faith allows you to transform challenges and adversity from obstacles into life lessons that you grow from. Sometimes you only find solutions to what you're facing by asking yourself the most difficult questions imaginable. Personal development should be an ongoing process and life practice, regardless of whether

## Introduction

you're an entrepreneur or you currently can't see yourself ever running a business. Your greatest strength often appears in moments that seem like life's lowest points.

While I was struggling through some of the most difficult moments of chemotherapy in the early years of *Fidelis*, the model that our team built allowed multiple people to change their lives. Cleaning operatives who worked two hours a day while their kids were at nursery are now senior managers earning almost 50% more than the average UK wage (across all sectors) and driving company cars. Some of the first people we worked with accepted part of their earnings in equity and have never regretted their decision.

So many business owners focus on their own vision and their own story. They dream of winning awards, getting hundreds of 'likes' on social media and cashing huge cheques. It's never just you on stage though. Great successes are powered by team effort and everyone on your team sharing in the success you've created together. In 2021, *Fidelis* employed 480 people. I will always remain grateful to each and every one of those team members for their relentless hard work and the happy faces that greeted me every day.

I'm also enormously grateful to my family and my life partner, Naomi, for supporting me through everything. You need a support system to overcome challenges. If you aren't able to open up to someone and let them open up to you, those things that are holding you back will stay locked inside you and will keep blocking your progress. Surrounding yourself with people who love you for the right reasons and want the best for you is vital for radiating happiness all around you. Life is a wonderful thing, don't spend so much of it in your own world that you forget to appreciate the wonders of the world around you.

This book is for anyone who wants to know what it takes to overcome adversity. Every challenge is manageable and no problem is permanent. Having a clear plan, not just for your business but for your life too, can show you a path forwards in the darkest of times. Knowing and determining your destination or destiny will undoubtedly help you to find the light at the end of the tunnel. Hopefully my experiences including not just the good but also the bad and the truly horrific can help you to reframe setbacks as the beginning of new successes. More importantly, I would like to help those of you who may have lost your faith in humanity to regain it. Entrepreneurs may find this book particularly interesting given my long business experience. However, I hope that anyone reading can find something that makes them smile and reflect on their own values and beliefs in these pages.

Reading never fails to cheer me up. Books provide phenomenal portals to other people's ideas, opinions and experiences. You will always learn something new whenever you pick-up a new book. I feel hugely privileged that people would read my book in the hope of improving their lives, professional careers and businesses.

Amazing people are everywhere. Find them, hire them, bring them into your team and most importantly of all, be a good friend to them. Everyone has influence. Use yours to spread positivity. Whenever you talk to someone, you're impacting their mood. From the first day of founding *Fidelis* in 2011, the whole team agreed to a courtesy system which required everyone to:

"Speak as if a person you're talking about was listening to your conversation, even if they're not in the room with you."

Office politics don't do anyone any good whatsoever. They just create negativity, weaken business culture and ultimately, wipe money off any future valuation of your business. More generally, talking negatively just brings you and those around you down. So many people will wonder why they always feel down and then spend 90% of their time complaining about everything and everyone. Progress starts from within. Focus on the positives in your life and go from there.

## Success leaves clues...

Always choose to help people whenever you can. That's everything that my current work revolves around. Part of that work is in consulting around Mergers and Acquisitions (M&A), helping business owners in facilities management to achieve the best value on their business sale that they possibly can. This can sometimes mean advising them to broaden their services offerings or improve their client experiences in order to maximise their company's final sale price.

The opportunity to move into M&A (mergers and acquisitions) came about as having helped us to sell *Fidelis*, one of their sector's most wonderful firms approached me to join them as a partner and to add my expertise to their facilities management offering. You

## Introduction

don't have to reinvent the wheel to create a great business and we all know that success leaves clues. If something's worked for another entrepreneur, then you can always apply that winning formula to your business model too. There are times when we have a duty to let some business owners know the truth and the disappointing news that they're not ready to sell yet. That's just the right thing to do. I'd rather help entrepreneurs to get the best possible result on a sale and help them to prepare their business for that success rather than persuade them to sell earlier for less just to net myself a quick commission.

Investment in experienced and 'been there' advice is vitally important for helping entrepreneurs to navigate the complexities of the due diligence process that is a pivotal part of any business sale. Initial due diligence and the surety that the buyer is serious in taking the process further is key to a fair and non-protracted process. This approach reaps real rewards for sellers and a fair deal for the buyer as both can trust that the other's claims and intentions are backed up by solid numbers. Sadly, there are some advisors who will rush this essential due diligence process and focus on what's in it for them rather than their clients' best interests. This just gives them a reputation for not doing the right thing when it really counts. Reputation is absolutely everything in business, especially when you're in the business of dealing with people's livelihoods and future lifestyles. Protect your reputation at all costs.

## Grow as an entrepreneur…

As you grow as an entrepreneur, you realise that the more success you can create for those around you, the more successful you'll become yourself. I will always go out and meet potential business buyers on behalf of my clients to see that they are a good fit for the culture of the company they're proposing to buy. Will they keep many of the existing staff in place? Will buyers treat cleaning operatives respectfully? Will current staff feel happy working under the new owners? These are all questions that matter hugely to me. All sellers know that any potential buyers I propose to them are the real deal because I've already sold two of my own multi-million pound businesses. Two co-owners came to me looking to sell their awesome business for £3 million. My support helped them to secure a £4.3 million final sale price which was fair and

## No Problem is Permanent

beneficial to both parties. Go out, talk to people, build relationships and look to always be honest, fair and trustworthy. That's how you win. If you leave your rose-tinted spectacles locked away in a drawer, you could be missing out on so many of life's rewarding and fulfilling opportunities.

My consultancy work these days also gives me the opportunity to teach, mentor and help leaders of integrity to achieve extraordinary results. Whether delivered 1-1 or with teams in their businesses, my support encourages both teams and business owners to confront the causes of any challenges they may face and grow through them. Anybody I work with can trust me to be there whenever they need me. To this day, I still receive calls from colleagues I mentored decades ago. Sharing in their growth is such a joy.

Thankfully, business success has allowed me to provide my hugely supportive family with the wonderful home life they've always deserved. I'm looking out of the window as I'm typing this now thinking about how it all began. Hindsight is a wonderful thing and I wish I could have changed so much about what I valued and how I related to other people in those first few years of my business career. However, mistakes are as indelible a part of life as successes. If you never put a foot wrong, you'll never learn how to put one right. My first real memories of life are of the half-asphalted streets around the housing estate in Chelmsley Wood (just outside Birmingham) where I grew up. I had a wonderful childhood. We had loads of love but never much money. The ability to start earning drove my first steps into the world of work. Did I know that I would become a business owner? No. Did I anticipate employing 480 people later in life? Absolutely not. I just got going. At twelve years old, I had a job with a milkman 7 days per week at 4:00 am in the morning and then on to two paper rounds before going to school. At 15, I decided to leave school and turn my earnings into a wage. Then I got my first job in a production bakery which made 15-20,000 loaves per hour.

Hard work and vision will help you jump over any hurdle in life..........

# Chapter One

## Enterprising beginnings

"You've got to work your socks off for anything and even then, nothing's guaranteed."

My family made the importance of honesty and hard work very clear to me from an early age. Money was always tight growing up and the council housing estate where we lived wasn't a great area to live in as the 1970's became the early 80's. Unemployment was high and you really had to put yourself out there and work hard to get anything. My Granda had served his country in the Second World War before returning home and eventually running his own business in Norfolk. Then, after moving up to Birmingham to explore new opportunities and reconnect with other family members, he built a career in a local production bakery.

My Dad worked hard there too, putting in 16-18 hour days to ensure that we had everything we needed growing up. Unfortunately, he had to retire at 55 due to ill-health. Mom worked 9am-2pm every day as the main receptionist for a local facilities management firm. I was always motivated to earn money and started working as soon as I was able. When many of my friends at school were sleeping, I was delivering milk and newspapers to bring some extra money into the house. When others might have been studying, relaxing or playing sports in the afternoons, I took extra shifts. Working was more than just a series of jobs to me. It felt like the only way to get the things I wanted most in life.

I remember that kids in school would always say, "Lloyd, why do you have so much cash on you?"

My answer was always, "Because I work for it."

While you can't control how your life begins, you can decide how it ends and create your own destiny. If you give up on having any ambition, you'll never grow into the person you could become. You can either accept defeat or fight adversity to build something awesome for yourself. That was why it was so difficult for me to justify spending time studying when I could spend the same amount of time earning money that would make a real difference to my life. It was only later in life that I wished I'd spent more of my teenage years studying. Those maths lessons come in handy when you're responsible for hundreds of people's jobs.

Unfortunately, I ended up learning many lessons through pretty awful experiences. That's one of the reasons why I made it easy for my teams to learn while they earnt when I became a business owner later in life. In my school years though, I was thinking far more about how much was in my back pocket than how many years King George III reigned for. Work seemed the only way to solve the adversity I faced at the time. Finding work was easy for me, even at such a young age, because I quite literally got on my bike and found a newsagent who would give me a paper round or two.

## Attitude over aptitude....

Our society is full of people who like to complain about the difficulties of getting a job or how their job doesn't pay them enough to go on the holidays they want. Despite never having much money, our parents always found the money to take us on holiday. Hard work takes you to your destination, wherever it may be. Social media helps hugely in getting there by providing opportunities to promote yourself professionally that weren't possible even ten years ago. Sometimes though, even in the social media era, you still have to knock on doors and pick-up the phone to find work.

Very often, using social media to amplify the great things that you're doing in real-life is key to making new audiences aware of

Enterprising beginnings

your skills and talents. Just sitting next to your phone or laptop, pressing post and hoping for the best is not going to get you to where you want to be anytime soon. I would say to all young people who are frustrated with the current economy to ask themselves if they've really done everything they possibly can to find more work. Have they called people up? Have they sent letters to different businesses with a well-designed CV? Have they dropped their CV into different offices? Have they really thought carefully about whether their CV separates them from all the other applicants for a job?

Graphic design agencies still tell me about people sending them CVs as Word documents in 12-point fonts. A lot of candidates also focus their preparation for job applications mostly on the interview stages. Of course, these interviews are vitally important parts of application processes but they are far from the only ones. Think about what you're applying for and whether every pre-interview aspect of your application, from your CV's covering letter right through to how you come across over the phone shows exactly why you'd do amazingly well in the role too. If you do the things that other applicants aren't doing then your talent and dedication will always shine through. Sometimes you need to think like an entrepreneur even if you don't run a business. Stand out, be positive and good things will happen.

Be reliable too. Failing to turn up to interviews or even work without giving appropriate notice and apologies will do nothing to further your career. This seems like such a basic thing that it shouldn't need to be said. Yet the amount of people who misunderstand work-life balance as not showing up for work is truly shocking. Be like an entrepreneur and turn up early for any agreed appointment, shift or day in the office. Apart from showing respect to whoever you're meeting, you'll give yourself a great opportunity to mingle and build relationships that will only boost your career.

People won't wait for you. You must show them why they were right to believe in you and give you opportunities to improve your life. Always ensure that you make eye contact with people too. Too often, younger people look at their phones when they're in the middle of a conversation. That just looks disinterested and risks you being quickly forgotten. If you listen to people, give them your full attention and ask interesting questions, they won't forget you. All entrepreneurs know that a great question and a firm handshake can make all the difference between sealing deals and reflecting on unsuccessful pitches. Great attitudes can always make up for knowledge gaps. Aptitude doesn't hold much value on its own.

## A winning mindset...

The first time I thought like an entrepreneur came after a few months of consistent paper rounds. Every Christmas, I would always knock on my customers' doors, wish them a Merry Christmas, and give them a hand-signed card. They all knew me by name and tipped very generously. I encountered my first entrepreneurial challenge when other lads didn't appreciate me slipping my cards into their customers' papers and then knocking on their doors to introduce myself. That issue nearly saw me get knocked off my bike.

I was completing a cover round one day and heard a booming voice behind me: "LLOYD, those are my customers, back off right now!"

Ignoring this voice didn't help. Luke just got angrier and angrier. Then, he started chucking stones at my bike. After the first one flew through the air and spun off my wheel, I got off my bike and walked straight up to him. Most people in that situation would have absolutely decked him, but I realised that would cost both of us our paper rounds.

"Don't do that to me EVER!" I shouted, completely fuming. "If they prefer my delivery style over yours then that's YOUR problem."

At that point, Luke taught me a hugely valuable lesson. "Actually, Lloyd, they're my customers and you're well out of order for trying to pinch them!"

To be fair, he had a point. My ambition had led me to step on his turf without asking and that wasn't a sustainable approach. I needed a way to keep these customers but lose all the aggro. The solution was to offer Luke and the other lads a 'commission' rather than their customers' tips. All that aggro disappeared when I started giving them in commission more than what they'd previously got in tips. Everything was about a deal. I wasn't just there to make a few extra quid but learnt that I needed to rein the sharp elbows in a bit.

In today's high-technology and globalised world, young people can gain the skills needed to become even more

# Enterprising beginnings

commercially savvy than my generation by improving their aptitude in foreign languages, computer technology, software engineering, geography and science. If they set up their own businesses, boosting these skills will massively improve their deal-making skills and the international markets they can access. If students in the UK use other countries' technologies without fully understanding how these technologies work and the contexts in which these innovations work best, then they'll be on the back foot throughout their careers. My focus all those years ago was always to build-up a loyal customer base who would stick with me. I managed to do that, but missed out on learning lots of things that would have proved very useful later in life.

A hugely valuable lesson that I did learn though was that sharp elbows won't get you far in business. It's crucial to compete with other entrepreneurs but also to build mutual relationships of respect with them. You don't want to be surrounded by hostile businesses who see their own success in ending yours. If you create a way for your growth to still allow some space in the market for your competitors to operate then everyone makes at least some money. Every industry benefits from innovation, whether you're talking about newspaper delivery, facilities management, food production or anything else. Present your innovations as ways that everyone wins and then you may even be able to absorb some of your biggest competitors into your operations.

Always go the extra mile too, not just for your customers but also for yourself and your family. Those who clock-off as soon as possible rarely advance into senior leadership roles or go on to start their own successful businesses. My determination to go the extra mile extended into my first job as a labourer at the production bakery. Some people would have gone home straight after a 7pm-7am shift on Saturdays and Sundays, but I was determined to learn and earn as much as I possibly could. An opportunity came up to stay for a few hours the next morning and work with the hygiene team to earn a bit more money. I did exactly that and became a skilled cleaning operative very quickly.

You often only know how to maintain world class service levels as an entrepreneur after completing work to excellent standards as a valued colleague and team member first. I had to learn how to clean meticulously, safely and efficiently in hazardous environments in order to progress in my career at the bakery. If the bakery hadn't been able to open later in the day,

## No Problem is Permanent

labourers would have missed out on shifts and pay, smaller bakeries would have gone unsupplied, and supermarket shelves would have gone empty. People who didn't even know me were relying on me to do a top job so that they could do theirs. One mistake would have seen me sacked and that just wasn't an option I could contemplate.

My desire to earn more and more money pushed me to become the best I could possibly be at anything I was asked to do. These days you can learn all sorts online, but no video tutorial can make up for getting stuck in with real on-the-job experience. Although I didn't see myself as a business owner back then, the service levels we offered at *Fidelis* would never have been possible without my early experience of spotlessly cleaning that bakery in a hurry.

Despite only being 18, my success at the bakery meant that I was able to buy my family very nice presents and still managed to save up quite a lot of money. At 17, I bought my first house before reaching the legal age to formally take possession of it – a huge achievement. Cleaning the production bakery had evolved into travelling around the country working all hours cleaning asbestos out of cellars. Despite the increased income, life working at the bakery was frustrating me. Some of my colleagues only showed up to pick-up a pay packet and leave. Their attention to detail was lacking in many areas and I felt that I couldn't provide the life that my then wife Tracey and young son Ian deserved unless I changed jobs.

An opportunity came up in Cambridge and I enthusiastically accepted what I thought would be a life-changing opportunity. Sadly, it didn't work out that way. Work continued to take up almost all of my time, my marriage to Tracey broke down and the new house we had only recently bought was put up for sale. I was so focused on earning more and more money that I didn't communicate sensitively and effectively with those around me. While there were many reasons for the end of our marriage, that didn't help.

When I was young and had ambitious financial goals, I just pursued them and didn't think about much else. At that point, my biggest goal was to become a millionaire by the age of 30. The world had felt like my oyster. Now the world seemed set against me. More experience in life and business taught me that developing and enjoying excellent relationships with those around you is far more important than adding zeroes to your pay. I still deeply regret not showing enough appreciation to my cousins who put me up in Cambridge while I was there. My whole self-esteem was centred around work and I didn't make anywhere near enough time for other things and people in my life. I didn't even send them a card saying thank you – how bad is that? While I would encourage all young people to work hard and be driven, I would say that those concepts apply to your personal life too. Think about any areas of your life that you would like to improve and try to set some targets for improvement every thirty days. These targets might just involve calling people, visiting them or writing them a card to show them how grateful you are for their support. All the money in the world won't make up for the feelings of loneliness you get if you don't have that support network around you.

Always remember that respect costs nothing.

# Fulfilment isn't fast...

Nowadays, I ask all my mentoring clients to complete '*The Circle of Life*' exercise to increase their happiness and fulfilment. The purpose of this exercise is to be able to display the different aspects of their lives in segments to clarify the intentions behind their goals and outcomes. This encourages clients to reflect on the whole of their lives and whether their current goals will actually help them to get what they want out of their futures.

Unfortunately, it was exactly this level of reflection that I lacked in Cambridge. Everything that possibly could have gone wrong did go wrong and I just became more and more upset. An end to my job there and my divorce from Tracey came in quick succession. Then I moved back into my parents' house for two years. It was so disappointing to have ended up right back where I started after working so hard to create a completely different life for myself and my son than I'd experienced when growing up. Associating all of my success with work and not really investing time in personal development outside of my job made this all the more difficult for me.

A period of immense depression followed.

I would just sit in the pub drinking alone. When the pub closed, I would go home and drink more. Working so hard had left me with few friends and I had gone from being hugely successful to alone and uncertain of my future in just a few short months.

Everyone has ups and downs with their mental health. If you are feeling like this, don't keep your feelings to yourself and definitely don't try to drink your problems away. Find someone who you can talk to about your feelings. At the time, I put all of my feelings into work and got a new job with my family's new cleaning business. Unless I took control of my life and started moving forwards then it seemed like things would only get worse for me. My parents were hugely encouraging and gave me incredibly generous support as I recovered my self-esteem and began to rebuild my life post-divorce. The house I'd owned with Tracey finally sold and we agreed cordial arrangements for me to regularly spend quality time with Ian. This hugely increased my confidence and turned sadness about the past into optimism for the future.

# Get over it...

I would encourage anyone going through adversity such as a divorce to try to reach a cordial agreement with your counterpart as soon as possible. That draws a definitive line under everything and allows you to move on and start rebuilding your life. While you might be entering a much less prosperous future than you were hoping for, don't dwell too much on this. Just focus on moving on. Keeping disagreements and arguments with your counterpart rumbling on and on does nobody any good whatsoever. It took me a very long time to accept that my marriage to Tracey was over before formalising our divorce. That led to a huge number of poor decisions and mistakes that I'm not proud of today. If you let adversity get the best of you then you'll spend all your time filled with anger and sadness. Only by seeing adversity as an uncomfortable but inevitable part of life that everybody goes through can you get through these moments. If you see obstacles as jumpable hurdles, they stop being immovable barriers between you and your success.

If only I'd seen life like this in those early days of my business career. After a very difficult process and with cash in the bank from the house sale, I was able to start thinking out of the box for new ways to grow the family business. They had won a large cleaning contract with the *Dairy Crest* factory near to where we lived. *Dairy Crest* was one of the region's best-known brands and biggest producers of milk. They needed to constantly have people

## Enterprising beginnings

available to work shifts. Unfortunately for them, they just didn't have the capacity to fill those shifts and were struggling with productivity. I came up with the concept of 'labour on loan' to solve their problem. If they were short staffed, they could hire some of our staff to work those shifts. This proved hugely successful and made a lot of money for the family business. Again though, my entire definition of success was driven by money. I didn't think much about much else at the time. I just found something I was great at and focused on that. Those early entrepreneurial experiences while at school had transformed into major deals that were creating jobs, paying wages, and building my reputation as an expert deal-maker. As I would soon find out though, dealmaking is only one part of business. If everything else in an organisation isn't aligned on the same growth trajectory, things can go south very quickly...

# Chapter Two

## Ambition on loan

"I was just wondering what kind of bonus I can expect this year?" was a question that I thought would get a very positive answer after the success of *'labour on loan'*.

I'd hoped that the initiative would send the family business skyrocketing. The answer I got from one of my relatives was the complete opposite of what I'd expected.

"Lloyd, how can you even ask that? You know there's barely enough money to pay your salary let alone a bonus."

Mismanagement had meant that the *Dairy Crest* work was propping up the whole business. Other invoices for completed projects went unpaid and were only ever half-heartedly chased up by lazy external 'debt collectors'. To make matters worse, new clients were even rarer than bonuses. Sadly, I had to leave the business to find personal and professional fulfilment. Leaving another family member's business is always an enormously tough decision but looking back my departure from the business seemed inevitable from the moment I joined. Anyone with an entrepreneurial mindset will know that growth is not just a goal for them; it's essential to their sense of purpose and wellbeing. It doesn't have to be purely financial growth either. Any advances in their lives, careers or personal relationships as a direct result of something that they've built qualify as growth. There's no fixed set of ideas driving entrepreneurs' thinking. Every business owner approaches challenges and opportunities differently.

So long as you're happy and you feel as though your life is moving forwards, you're making progress. There's absolutely nothing wrong with thinking about businesses that you might start and then waiting (even for a number of years) before launching that idea into the world. If you think you've got an idea that could make an amazing business, flesh it out a bit into a plan and have a chat with those you trust the most. Then, when the time is right, you can start putting your plan into action. There is no set time frame for this but if you are waiting for the perfect time to come it never will. You will know when you are ready and that's when to get started. When the moment to become an entrepreneur comes, you'll know.

# Learning to love yourself...

Don't beat yourself up if that moment doesn't catapult you to success either. If becoming a millionaire was easy, then everyone would be one. Business success requires patience and, almost inevitably, failure before landing on that one brilliant idea and plan. I've failed more than a few times in search of profitable and sustainable business models. Everyone fails at some point in business. Those who share posts in front of 'their new' flash *Harley Davidson* motorbike only a few weeks after launching their first business almost certainly asked their Mum's permission to take pictures with her *Harley* before posting.

The most important thing in life and in business is that we all love ourselves: win, lose or draw. This is massively difficult for some people to even contemplate, let alone do. Sometimes loving ourselves means taking risks, just so we can tell ourselves that we gave ambitions we'd always had a proper go. A fear of missing out can eat away at us far more than a fear of failure. On the other hand, loving ourselves might also mean that we're much happier when taking no risks at all. Many people across the world hold a job down for most of their lives and live happily. They have absolutely no interest in all the uncertainty that entrepreneurship brings into life.

# No Problem is Permanent

Whatever you do in life, feeling good within yourself (not just about yourself) matters the most. Feeling good about yourself is crucial as it means that you feel positive about everything that you're doing in the moment. Feeling good within yourself is deeper. It means feeling like you're achieving your long-term purpose and being at peace with yourself too. In a professional context, it relates more to how you feel about your overall career trajectory than your current role. Mental health and wellbeing at work is talked about a lot but often only in relation to workload management. While a good work-life balance is a great benefit to our overall health, pressure from deadlines is not the only area where mental health impacts our professional lives. Work, whether employed or self-employed, should help us to pursue our own goals rather than just being something that we feel obliged to do every day. If you feel like you're not progressing in your role, you might just be in the wrong job. Think about what you could learn, what you could create and what extra value you could add in a different role that would give you a more fulfilling life personally as well as professionally.

Initially, I thought I could get all the professional fulfilment that I would ever need in life by working at the bakery. The job seemed like a road to riches in the beginning. There was no shift I wouldn't take and no site I wouldn't visit if it meant me picking up a larger pay packet each week. Then everything suddenly went downhill. I was back at my childhood home urgently seeking a way out, so took the first opportunity I could. The money that I'd enjoyed in recent years had gone and it seemed as though I was back at square one. My emerging-inner businessman needed to make money quickly, move back into my own place and return to a progressive career trajectory after the seemingly dream job in Cambridge fell apart.

Thankfully, a new role and a new sense of purpose came. Those entrepreneurial instincts which had helped me to corner the market in local newspaper deliveries in my school days and had then given me the motivation to travel around the country cleaning were about to take on a whole new form. I was about to realise how good at business development I could become. Those skills and self-conditioning would be crucial in building successful businesses later in life. Before all that though, my first role at the family business was as a cleaning supervisor. At the time, everything was looking up and my biggest hope was to stay with the family business long-term. The supervisor role involved both cleaning and managing a small team. One of the directors brought me in to work on their main contract with *Dairy Crest* as that work was the business' principal source of revenue. They couldn't take any chances.

Staying as a supervisor long-term was never going to be enough for me; I wanted more and was determined to get it. Firstly though, it was important to get to grips with the role and prove that the director hadn't made a mistake in bringing me onboard. On showing me around the site on my first day, their final words before leaving me to it were, "Don't let us down!"

After finishing my cleaning work to the highest standard every day, I learnt as much as I could about how the facilities management sector worked at the time. There was much to improve on. For example, clients were regularly referred to as 'contracts'. This terminology framed the client relationships as purely transactional: we cleaned, they paid. This clearly wasn't the way to go. Businesses are built by people and the relationships that the family business had with *Dairy Crest*'s managers and directors would be decisive in determining whether we would become their long-term facilities management partners or not.

# Strong relationships build strong businesses...

I quickly paid a colleague to complete my cleaning work and concentrated on developing my relationships with *Dairy Crest*'s top team. This was my first real experience of creating a professional network. Networking doesn't always have to take place at events. They help lots, but ultimately networking is just about building relationships and teams capable of creating value. I was already the *Dairy Crest* managers' main contact from the family business on site so had plenty of opportunities to enjoy quality conversations with them and expand our business relationships.

After another busy day, I popped into their office to see how things were going and one of their managers, Jim, said, "I'd love to go and watch the *Villa*. We can never get tickets and listening to the match on the radio just isn't the same. The dairy is only just down the road from *Villa Park* too."

## No Problem is Permanent

This gave me an idea. *Villa Park* was *Aston Villa Football Club*'s stadium, and it had been a regular feature of my weekends for longer than I could remember. It only made sense to sort the *Dairy Crest* managers out with tickets for their favourite home games. After some persuading, the family business bought four of the Club's season tickets for *Dairy Crest*'s top team to enjoy. Giving them my season ticket to fill a seat when I couldn't make the game wasn't going to be enough. The extra tickets meant that managers could share home match tickets amongst themselves and take their families to the games too. They all constantly wanted the tickets and I suddenly became the most popular person in the office. Everyone suddenly started getting me chocolates, wine and all sorts of gifts. To avoid hurting anybody's feelings and keep things fair, we had to create a ticket schedule. Nobody in the facilities management sector had really seen corporate hospitality as a meaningful way of building business relationships - until then. Pioneering this method of client entertainment was one of the best decisions that the family business ever made. It was also my first step in applying what I'd learned over the years to try to push the sector forwards.

Conversations in the office usually went something like "What an atmosphere at the game! My kids had the best time, and we have you to thank for that, Lloyd."

I'd then respond by talking about anything but work. We'd talk about football, family and almost every other topic apart from politics or religion. When I was chatting to the *Dairy Crest* managers first thing on a Monday morning, my job was not to sell. It was to earn their trust and make sure that I was the first person they spoke to about business issues later in the day. Then my job changed to understanding how our business could better solve the challenges they faced with the resources we had available. That would create more value for them and therefore mean more business for us too. They started to tell me about gaps in their rotas where their people were suddenly unavailable for shifts.

"Young Tom's skived off again and we're short-staffed" or "Danny's ill, can you find someone to cover?" were regular comments.

Hundreds of shops depended on the dairy for their deliveries of fresh milk in trendy new plastic bottles. Production dropping simply wasn't an option. *Dairy Crest*'s bosses were very concerned about this and didn't know what to do. That was when I suggested *'labour on loan'*. Our people would get some extra

## Ambition on loan

money for covering some of *Dairy Crest*'s shifts, and production volumes would stay high: everybody won. *Dairy Crest* agreed to pay our negotiated rates for every operative who covered a shift, allowing us to significantly increase revenue from our original deal with them without reducing our capacity.

Following the success of *'labour on loan'*, the *Dairy Crest* team came to me to solve challenges which hadn't even existed when I began my business career. Plastic milk bottles had just hit the market and were made in what was called the 'blow room'. The process of making these bottles required expert usage of highly complex equipment. We were entering the first era of mass automation in the manufacturing industry; what was new then would be considered an historical artefact nowadays. However, at that time it was absolutely crucial that the *Dairy Crest* team could use the latest technology available to produce as many bottles as possible every day. Otherwise, they would miss out on countless sales. Unfortunately for *Dairy Crest*'s managers, their staff lacked the training needed to use all that new machinery quickly and effectively.

One day, Jim pulled me aside and said, "Lloyd, if we can't fill our company skills gap in using these machines, then we won't be able to service 40% of our orders. If that happens, the business could go under."

Like so many businesses, the *Dairy Crest* managers had taken on orders without having the right people in place to fulfil them. Fortunately, I was able to come to the rescue and in the end, the managers just outsourced all of the 'blow room's' maintenance and productivity to us. That's how integral the family business had become to their operations: largely thanks to my relationship building and that first, very successful venture into corporate hospitality.

From bottle manufacturing, we were then asked to do the deep cleans of the newly created workspaces across the dairy. Then a contract to manage *Dairy Crest*'s grounds and even a window cleaning deal followed. What had started as client relationship management had become something far bigger. At the same time, my own professional network was expanding almost as much as our order book. The *Dairy Crest*'s Site Director became a close personal friend, as did Ray, their Head of Security. Ray was not always the most popular of people on site, but we got on brilliantly.

## No Problem is Permanent

I remember speaking to him one day and he said, "People think I'm harsh, but I'm just obsessed with high standards. Any security issues on site and the whole dairy will have to shut for at least a day. Do you have any idea how much that would cost us? We'd have to let people go!"

As it happened, I did, and I was determined to fully support him in maintaining world-class standards on site and promoting strong growth. That helped me to secure great new great jobs for many of my talented friends. Ray always trusted everyone I brought on site which made that process easy. He didn't like football, so I would always bring him small gifts to take home to his family as a token of my appreciation. The jobs then just kept on coming.

Friends I'd grown up with would offer me money to secure their preferred shifts for them. I'd get them the shifts anyway and never took a penny from them: it was their hard-earned money, after all. I even managed to get a friend who was an excellent mechanic hired as the *Dairy Crest*'s official mechanic. What mattered most to me was moving my whole community forwards. Anyone who's willing to put the graft in should have the chance to show what they can do in any role. You never know where your best-ever hire might come from. My friends repaid the favour and gave me a wide network of skilled and loyal professionals who I could still count on to work with me on different sites many years later. When you're setting up your own business, the ability to rely on this type of trusted professional network can make the difference between profitability and huge losses. At the time, when I was mainly focused on generating extra revenue for the family business, I didn't truly understand the full extent of how valuable the community built in those early years of networking would become later on.

Growing my network has only increased in importance throughout my career. After that productive first experience of building relationships across a growing team, it's amazing that I felt so nervous when speaking about my own business at networking events in later years. Speaking about my business for the first time in front of those large audiences was one of the scariest things I ever did. Then I spoke about my business so many times that it became normal, and those rooms full of people became great personal friends. Whenever you try anything new, always try to break it down into different stages. Then work out which parts you've done before and go from there. For example,

## Ambition on loan

you might not have spoken to a large audience before, but you've definitely spoken to more than one person about your work before and built a relationship with them. Do that at scale and you're well on your way to building a great professional network, whether you attend many events or not. The bigger the network you have, the easier it will be to make those crucial first connections if, like I did, you decide to launch your own business after successfully growing someone else's.

Your network can help you to feel happier and more confident too. Talking to trusted professional peers about whether ideas might work can give you a good sense of where you can be successful and where's best to avoid. As a result, you lower your risk of plunging time and money into things that might not work so well. You can offer them the same advice and grow together. If you're in similar sectors you can refer each other business too. Facilities management firms and construction firms will always have projects that they can share. The same goes for larger marketing agencies and copywriters. If you can build strong relationships with people whose clients will need your services, then business development becomes a whole lot easier than you might have first thought.

Investing time into relationship-building shows people how much you care about their success too. In today's society, it's so easy just to send someone a message, call them, engage with a social media post and think you've done enough to build a productive professional relationship with them. Life, both at home and at work, is about so much more than just pressing buttons though. If you want to earn a professional counterpart's trust, then you've got to consolidate relationships built through different communications channels and invest time in meeting them in-person multiple times. There's nothing quite like spending time with people in the flesh for building strong long-term professional relationships. You also need to listen closely to the challenges they're facing so that you can help them to find the solutions eluding everyone else. That's why I was so keen to secure as much face-time with *Dairy Crest*'s managers and directors as possible. It was the only way to innovate new services capable of adding substantial value to their business.

No Problem is Permanent

# Focus on solving customers' pain, not selling stuff...

When you're trying to sell products and services to clients, sell solutions to the issues causing them hassle rather than things. Marketing agencies refer to these hassles as 'pain points'. The more you can solve, the easier clients' lives become and the more they value your support.

Years later, when pitching the services of my own business, prospects regularly asked me:

"Why do we need professional cleaning?"

My response was always:

"We'll take the hassle out of cleaning your business. That all helps you to run your business more efficiently and boost productivity. On those nights where you're feeling too tired to clean and just want to go home, our operatives will make sure that your colleagues and clients walk into fresh and tidy spaces in the morning."

The service that I was pitching then stopped being a service. It transformed into an easy route for business owners to achieve their own goals: saving time and making money. They could tell me they weren't interested, but then they'd have to wait much longer to hit their performance targets, because everyone works better and feels better in pristine spaces.

Products and services are temporary: they can be picked up and then dropped just as quickly. Solutions that help people towards their goals are long-term and allow suppliers to guarantee revenue from clients over multi-year periods. That's how you build a business. All of my own businesses have benefited from long-term relationships and agreements with clients. I want them to feel value from any service I'm associated with for five years, not five months.

Sadly, the family business couldn't achieve this longevity, but nobody thought much about that as *labour on loan* took off. Everything seemed to be working out fantastically both for me personally and the business as a whole. Relations with *Dairy Crest* reached an all-time high and the entrepreneurial talent I'd always had seemed to be shining through. Sadly though, other things within the family business weren't going well at all. Every growing business needs a strong team culture to turn periods of

Ambition on loan

growth into sustainable business enlargement. Lots was happening behind the scenes but not much involved sharing values or staying on the same page. Team meetings often just disintegrated into unprintable rows as individuals – myself included - used their own successes as leverage to compete with colleagues rather than pooling their talents to create a stronger and more resilient business.

Some people were obsessed with old-fashioned business practices which treated clients poorly. The thought of partnering with clients to innovate rather than just selling to them seemed completely alien to them. Positioning yourself as a partner puts you in the top bracket of suppliers to any business. Suppliers can come and go, but partners stay by the side of businesses to help them achieve their long-term strategic goals. Better still, partners can ensure that any services they deliver or products they make for the businesses they work with are tailored to achieve exactly those goals. This significantly reduces the risk of those businesses wasting money on unsuccessful strategies. Partners then become the first people that businesses call when they need advice on particular issues. Being integral to business operations then puts those partners in pole position for agreement renewals when tenders come back into the market for public bidding. It also allows those partners to expand their own businesses into other areas, based on the needs of those they're collaborating with. Take '*labour on loan*' as an example. Most people might feel that cleaning operatives can't successfully cover labour shifts in a dairy because they're completely different jobs. There are those false assumptions kicking in again.

If you only see people as the jobs they work, then those kinds of barriers appear. If, instead, you see talented and motivated people who are willing to give new things a go, then you can help them to earn and learn more by covering a whole range of different shifts. This approach paid dividends later in my business career.

At *Fidelis,* a colleague passed me in the office and asked, "Lloyd, can I have a go at sales admin? You know that I'm trustworthy, good with people and hardworking. I think it would be fascinating to learn the processes involved in business development."

Many bosses would have shut her request straight down, but I was always eager to let my team improve their skills. We let Sam take on some more admin work and move into sales. We never looked back. She would achieve phenomenal things and go on to help us to add more than 7 figures worth of profitable business to the company. Giving people the opportunity to showcase their talents is one of the most wonderful things about being a business owner. An advantage of partnerships is that clients trust you enormously and that extends to them also trusting your judgement if you give a colleague the chance to try something new and learn new skills. Partnerships aren't perfect though. They occasionally go wrong because of complacency. Sometimes business owners who feel as though they are guaranteed business take continuations of relationships for granted. In the cleaning industry, that might look like not attending open events for tenders or not visiting sites to continue building relationships with clients. It might also look like not providing them with platforms to quickly and conveniently let you know how happy they are with the quality of work being done. Always treat any project like it's your first, even if it's your 1,000th. That way, you'll always show clients how much you appreciate your partnership with them and deserve their continuing trust.

Sadly, trust was in short supply between myself and some of my colleagues within the family business. There were too many different approaches to business-building within the team. A number of people saw themselves as the top producers in the business, despite the fact that they weren't the ones going out and building lucrative long-term client relationships. As the business grew, the revenue from my relationships at *Dairy Crest* couldn't subsidise everything. Months would pass until I discovered just how much the business was owed in unpaid invoices and just how much those paid to recover these long overdue debts had let the business down with their lacklustre efforts. The main thing I noticed at the time was that no matter how much extra revenue I brought in, my wages weren't increasing. I was still going home to my parents' house despite spending all day securing ever larger deals for the business.

# A new beginning...

One evening, I thought that the site was almost empty and was ready to finish for the day when a soft but confident voice came from the back of the room and asked me, "Lloyd, have you ever wanted more from life?"

## Ambition on loan

"Who hasn't?" was my eager reply, immediately clicking with the person standing opposite me.

We then had a fascinating conversation about life, the universe and almost everything in between. My to-be 2nd wife had just come into my life. Let's call her *M*. *M* worked part-time cleaning the *Dairy Crest* site and was coming out of a relationship in which she didn't feel truly fulfilled. She wanted more out of her career than her current role as a cleaning operative gave her, and like me, she was determined to create better opportunities for herself and her kids. The wonderful thing about the cleaning industry is that it gives anyone with the right attitude a chance to build better careers and lives for themselves. If you want an opportunity, this industry lets you take one. Anyone can learn how to progress in the industry if they have the right mindset and appropriate professional training. The attributes of attention to detail, diligence, friendliness and reliability that take people far in life are particularly crucial for success in this sector. If you show the right attitude you can progress from being a cleaning operative to a supervisor, right through to owning your own business. Then, you never know, you might even sell yours and then help others to sell theirs too.

All too often, cleaning is dismissed as a 'job' rather than a 'career'. It's as if people want to imply that cleaning won't get you anywhere in life. They then walk into the offices and hope that the cleaning team did an amazing job overnight because they have a hugely busy schedule of meetings that day. Imagine if the cleaning team decided that they'd all have a few days off that week: those meetings probably wouldn't go so well. Like any career, facilities management is what you make of it. There are opportunities to build wonderful lives for yourselves and your families. You just have to take them. *M* and I were determined to make the most of all the opportunities coming our way. Eventually, I would partner with *M* to set up my first business, *Keen Kleen*, which would grow to an impressive turnover. Long before that moment though, we decided to build a home together.

This was hugely complicated by the fact that *M* hadn't made herself hugely popular with the family. As much as my family's disapproval saddened me, creating a household with my new partner represented the growth that I'd sought for quite some time. Getting back on the property ladder and recovering from the trauma of my break-up from Tracey and everything that followed was an absolute priority. *M* and I were eventually able to buy a

## No Problem is Permanent

home and start a new life together. I was still working at the family business and felt more undervalued by the team there every day. False accusations were made, relationships with colleagues fell apart, and ultimately, I had to move on.

The constant cycle of working tirelessly without really pushing my life forwards in a meaningful way was beginning to get me down. Creating a home with M helped, but I still felt as though there was only so far that I could go within the family business. Other people in similar roles to me elsewhere were earning far more for the same work. I was leading the development of a major client relationship and needed to start seeing some pay-off from that work in my own life. Spirituality comes from different places for everyone and, at that time, mine involved building the best possible life that I could. Spirituality doesn't have to be religious. For many people, believing in a higher power and linking that belief to a series of principles set out in a religion helps them to give their life meaning. If that works for you, then great, but that's not the only way to give your life meaning. Overcoming challenges can often help you to find that meaning by putting the little things into perspective. Your spirituality can change over time too. Mine certainly did.

Some of the difficulties I faced later in my career made my challenges in managing the *Dairy Crest* contract look like just another day at the office. When you're having to overcome divorce, life-threatening illness and run a business simultaneously, you begin to ask what it's all really for. Then you realise that everything has an answer. There's no challenge in life that you can't solve, because no problem is permanent. So long as everything you do helps you and your family, you're one step closer to your goals. If you're not sure what those goals might be, then just focus on being a positive person in the moment and go from there. Probably the most important aspect of spirituality is what you as an individual put out into the world. Constant negativity just surrounds you with disappointment. Positivity answers, 'yes' when others say 'no' and always seeks improvements. You can make every day a great day if you approach it positively. If you're determined to create something better each day, then you will achieve exactly that. It doesn't have to be a huge thing. It could be anything.

You could make someone feel better by putting your busy day to one side and dropping in on one of your friends to see how they are. Positivity and purpose (when combined) turn dreams and

## Ambition on loan

ambitions into realities. Even if they might not admit it, the most successful people alive will often have some form of spirituality driving this powerful combination. Feeling as though you need to get somewhere to fulfil yourself gives you a determination to do whatever it takes which is unmatched by anything else in the world. Crucially, spirituality also helps you to remain in touch with the world around you. You can then find peace where others may only see chaos and drama.

I very much wish I'd considered spirituality in far more depth all those years ago. Unfortunately, my determination to just move on with my life overwhelmed any desire to reflect on the complexities of its meaning. In the end, my decision to become an entrepreneur alongside *M* came by chance. We were flicking through the *Birmingham Mail* and saw an advert that would change both of our lives forever. The advert was for cleaning franchises. It gave ambitious people the opportunity to build their own cleaning businesses without needing to incur massive costs. The sites on offer were prestigious too: a major bank, an enormous engineering factory and a well-known printer. I saw this as my first real opportunity to put my entrepreneurial skills to the ultimate test and start a business.

Sometimes huge moments in your life emerge from chance happenings. Many people would like to say that their decision to start a business was planned out for some time. That isn't always the case though. There are times in life where opportunities come and you just back yourself to propel yourself to a better life through them. The right mindset can take you to incredible places. Sometimes those places involve turning your job into a thriving business providing fantastic lifestyles for hundreds of people. If you've been thinking about starting a business and an opportunity comes up, take it. Yes, it will be the most difficult challenge you've ever taken on. Yes, there will be days where you question yourself. But with enough determination, you can make incredible things happen. Impossible is a state of mind. If you make your purpose to be a positive person and feel that in your soul, then the concept of impossibility transforms from a mental barrier to a figment of your imagination. You can then go beyond achieving your ambitions and surprise yourself with how much excellence you really can create.

And so that one advert led us to become franchisees. There was a huge problem though: paying for our franchises would involve losing 20% of our revenue each month. As a result, we didn't make any real money for almost a year and a half after taking the leap into our own venture. *Mr* Wheatley, as he insisted on being called, required the full amount to be paid every month and would not consider giving us any kind of flexibility or further credit. On reflection, that's just business and we shouldn't have expected anything else. At the time though, we leapt into franchise ownership without really knowing just how long it would take to start turning a profit. The entire cost of buying the franchise needed to be repaid in full and the sheer length of time that this debt took to pay off was an endless cause of frustration for both of us. There's nothing worse than spending hours grafting and then seeing all of your money disappear in bills before it's even been in your account for an hour. Earning extra revenue wherever and whenever possible became essential for both of us. As a result, we eventually went direct to different businesses and took on several new clients.

This presented a major challenge to our new boss, who urgently had to find a way to bring these new accounts under his brand. Mr Wheatley's response would shape the rest of my career…

# Chapter Three

## Chasing validation

I was driving back from signing our new deal with Mr Wheatley feeling happy but not quite ready to celebrate just yet. Something was gnawing away at me. As soon as I got home, I read back through our new contract and the full extent of what we'd just signed dawned on me. My mood came crashing back down to earth. The contract read something like this:

"*The franchisees agree to pay 20% of all payments they receive to the franchiser until all costs involved in acquiring the franchise have been reimbursed. They also agree to buy all of their supplies exclusively from the franchiser and will not attempt to negotiate any aspect of related costs with the franchiser.*"

## No Problem is Permanent

Pretty much every business owner will tell you that they've made at least one absolutely terrible deal at some point in their career. This was one of mine.

Buying franchises at the first opportunity seemed like the fastest route to removing myself from the growing tensions and difficulties engulfing the family business, while creating a better life for myself and Ian. Then reality struck! *M* and I had just signed ourselves up for at least two years in Mr Wheatley's debt. In plain English, the contract stated that on top of losing 20% of all our invoices for the foreseeable future, we also had to buy all of our materials from Mr Wheatley at whatever price he wanted to sell them to us.

So why did I sign a deal with him in the first place? The deal mattered so much to me at the time for two reasons. Firstly, the opportunity to build a business and eventually earn enough to invest in greater fulfilment for myself and my loved ones was an opportunity I couldn't turn down. Secondly, and most importantly, building that successful business would represent validation. The long-term payoff of proving myself right in moving away from the family business more than made up for less cash in the short-term. I wish I could write that some impressive mission statement about saving the world determined my decision to give self-employment a go. That might read nicely, but it wouldn't be true though. The pursuit of the validation that I'd sought for so long drove me to hand a massive chunk of my earnings every month over to Mr Wheatley in franchise fees.

There's nothing wrong with paying franchise fees. They present huge opportunities for people to launch their own businesses while giving franchise owners a fair return. However, there is a problem with constantly being in someone's debt, no matter how hard you work, because the deal you signed is geared in their favour. It quickly became clear to me that no matter how much business I generated for him, *Mr* Wheatley would never see or treat me as his equal. The only way for my new cleaning business to become profitable was for me to own the franchises outright and then, as my reputation improved, acquire clients directly without needing Mr Wheatley's assistance. The odds were stacked against me but what's not to love about a bit of adversity. Franchisees almost never bought full ownership of sites they were leasing back then due to sky high costs. This was the assumption behind Mr Wheatley's business model. It wasn't stated in the contract, but it was a fundamental part of his business plan. In his mind, his franchisees would never develop their own independent brands successfully enough to repay the fees and go on to acquire clients without needing his support. He fully expected to make a fortune off their work indefinitely. He was correct in assuming that most people would never work the hours needed to accomplish all of that.

However, he'd never met anyone like me before. Sadly, the accomplishment of eventually buying the franchise from him didn't feel as good as it should have done because, money aside, it took me a painfully long time to obtain the validation and appreciation that I was really searching for.

Nobody said, "Well done, Lloyd, that's an awesome achievement!" after my franchise purchase went through.

A few of the people I had worked with over the years almost seemed disappointed that my new venture hadn't gone up in smoke. Mr Wheatley was one of them, but he put his disappointment to one side as he looked for new ways to get and hang on to his cut of the revenues that I was generating.

Long before that moment arrived, there was a load of work to be done if I ever wanted to see 100% of the invoices I was billing land in my account again. Both myself and *M* were so determined to become successful and respected business owners that we worked shifts that nobody else was prepared to work. Our plan was to continue working at the family business until we had fully paid-off the franchise fees. Balancing the *Dairy Crest* work with our new franchisee roles required working 6am-1am almost every day for 18 months. This process was far more difficult than we ever imagined it would be, but sometimes your mind can take you to incredible places. Everyone has goals but far fewer people have the focus, determination and hard work required to achieve them. Thankfully, we did.

Unfortunately though, this difficult process was made even tougher by some completely unnecessary factors.

# A difficult departure...

Family businesses can often forget to separate the family from the business, making leaving them a far more arduous process than anyone needs. My initial decision to move away and join Mr Wheatley was met with shock. Why would I want to seek a better future elsewhere? Was the family not enough? Why did I not want

## No Problem is Permanent

them to share in my success? I had to face many questions like this for months after moving into franchising. None of them came near to landing my actual reason for leaving. Despite all the effort I'd put into expanding our relationships across teams at *Dairy Crest*, the family business was not growing into other sectors. We still weren't picking up many new clients, and, to make matters worse, the company's long-term cash flow problems had left us deep in arrears on our own bills. There had been too much focus on the present rather than the future when things were looking up and now, each day at work just seemed to find a way of being bleaker than the last one. On top of that, staff perks and wellbeing policies were unheard of back then. After a difficult period of reflection, it became clear to me that I wasn't going to achieve professional or personal growth unless I looked for pastures new. This sad conclusion wasn't a rejection of my family in any way. It was a rejection of some of the people working for them and advising them who had become too complacent and spent more time talking the talk than walking the walk. I was tired of going out of my way to help people who didn't make any attempt to show their appreciation for my efforts or consider any changes which might drive growth. Sometimes in life, you have to take decisions that make you hugely unpopular, even with yourself, in pursuit of your long-term goals. With the benefit of time and everyone's best friend, Captain Hindsight, there are always things that you'll wish you could have done differently in the past.

However, at the time, you're in the moment and everything's happening too quickly for you to feel in control of events. Someone tells someone something that they thought you said in a coffee break a few days ago, and suddenly, multiple relatives are offended over things that never actually happened. If you find yourself in this situation, you must accept that however clear you are about your intentions and however much you insist that your departure from the family business is nothing personal, some of the closest people to you will never understand. Worse still, they will always take everything personally. You might be able to rebuild relationships eventually, but this won't happen overnight. The most important thing is that you enter any venture you're involved in honestly and with a good heart. Even if people don't like the fact that you left the family business, they'll (hopefully) come to respect the fact that you've built a business on your own even if they don't tell you personally.

Chasing validation

Years after I'd fully left the family business, I remember overhearing my Dad telling his friends:
"Our Lloyd's done amazingly well, he's got a top of the range Merc and everything, I'm so proud of him."

He could never say that to me though. Backing yourself when it feels like some of those closest to you don't truly support your success is indescribably difficult.

This is another reason why proper business planning is so crucial. The difference between dwelling over emotional matters and pushing forwards is following a clear plan that sets out exactly how you'll create positive changes to your life and move closer to your goals step-by-step. Hoping for quick-fixes and shortcuts gets you nowhere. The same goes for arguments and negativity.

Try and avoid taking sides in the arguments that can so often consume family businesses and drag on for ages (even after you've left), marring the launch of your new business. Instead, surround yourself with people who are slightly removed from the situation and can appreciate that you're building something new and awesome. Being an entrepreneur doesn't have to be a lonely journey. The right support network can do wonders for both your mental health and your new company's growth.

Unfortunately though, in an effort to avoid feelings of loneliness, you sometimes surround yourself with people who don't in fact have your best interests at heart. I discovered that to my great cost many years later as *M* devastatingly proved to be one of those people. Life is a learning process and that applies to business life more than anything else. Along the road of your business journey, you'll meet amazing and inspiring people who remain friends for decades and help you to overcome adversity. Likewise, you can support them in the same way.

Always remember that a back-up plan is no bad thing either. Sometimes success can take a while to come and you'll need something to fall-back on in the meantime.

# A job isn't such a bad thing...

If you scroll through your social media feeds, you'll see many young entrepreneurs talking about jobs as if they're old-fashioned things from 20 years ago that unimaginative people did in a simpler time. You can find more sensible advice walking back from a party talking to an overworked and underpaid children's

## No Problem is Permanent

entertainer who is late for his second job and has no idea where he parked his car. The entertainer might aspire to make the world smile but realises that he needs another job too in order to support his loved ones. The most important thing in life is feeling fulfilled and pursuing your purpose. If your purpose is to make the world a happier place but also to support your kids, then you might want to follow the entertainer's example. Holding down a job while getting your business off the ground isn't, and should never be, portrayed as a sign of weakness. Rather it's a sign that you want to create the best possible life for your family, and don't want them to suffer if your passion takes a while to provide you with a sustainable income.

I've recently enjoyed listening to Curtis '*50 Cent*' Jackson's audiobook '*Hustle Harder, Hustle Smarter*', where he refers to business opportunities you pursue on the side of doing your regular job as '*side hustles*'. Each side hustle increases your income and becomes a positive revenue-building opportunity rather than a distraction. My side hustle became a successful business. However, if I had spent all my time working for Mr Wheatley, I would have lost thousands of pounds in potential revenue for years to come by remaining a franchisee for far longer. It was only by using the salary generated from my job with the family business that I was able to pay-off his franchise fees faster than he ever expected and begin to form what became *Keen Kleen*, while supporting Ian, *M* and her kids too.

Don't just leap into projects and end up investing colossal resources into side hustles that aren't on a path to delivering you some decent extra income or contributing positively towards your goals.

Whenever you start a new venture, think carefully about how much and how quickly it will contribute to your household income. If you work in an office job, avoid dancing around the office telling everyone that you're now an entrepreneur and theatrically resigning, only to need your job back a few months later.

Messages on work group chats like, "Just so you all know, I'm leaving tomorrow," can come over as cold or insensitive.

Equally, "I'm so sorry that you didn't follow my advice, but I wish the company all the best!" just looks rude.

Neither message will do much to secure you future work in the industry. Take time to talk to people in-person or message them individually (if you can't speak to them or meet-up with them).

Chasing validation

Tell them how much you enjoyed working with them and that you hope you can work together again soon.

Entrepreneurs still have bills to pay and sometimes that means putting your business idea on the back-burner and keeping your job for a bit longer than you'd hoped. That doesn't mean that you scrap the idea completely though. Just like watching a film or TV show, you only press pause when you want to come back to something later. Great ideas don't always have to be actioned immediately to become successes. Growth ideas might work even better if you spend time developing them. So much of business success is about timing. Waiting until you think that you've got a great opportunity to make an impact in your market before pressing play on your ideas can pay dividends. The thinking time this gives you will also help you to plan for making money in the worst-case scenario. If you can do that, then you can steer your business through anything. *Keen Kleen* wasn't in a position to be formally incorporated as a business until 2000. That was almost a decade after it started as my side hustle. Those years of development time gave us crucial tools to launch a limited company with a much greater chance of success. Patience really is a virtue when it comes to business planning.

Everyone's time is limited, so only pick side hustles that you're hugely passionate about and committed to. Having to do another day's work after finishing a busy day's work requires a drive that very few people can maintain consistently. Once you've picked your side hustle, structure it with a commercial outlook from the very beginning. If you approach a side hustle as a hobby, then it will always be a hobby. Focus on how you can turn your passion into reliable, high-quality products and services that people will buy. Write yourself a small business plan listing your expected costs, how much you (realistically) expect to make each year and then forecast your first year's profit. Invest time in marketing too. Marketing is about so much more than just flyers, adverts or social media posts. Marketing creates a connection between your products and services and your customers. When they buy from you, you want to sell them more than just a thing or your time. You want to sell them an idea, a lifestyle or a better way of doing things that will keep them coming back again and again.

Although this might sound complicated, it's actually very simple. Ask yourself some questions about why your products or services are so great. What makes them different from everything else on the market? How do they make people's lives easier? Then

## No Problem is Permanent

work out your target audience. Who will your business benefit most? Which groups of people in society need your help and why? Then look at how you'll speak to those people. Think about the lifestyles they live and where your business fits into their typical days. Then you'll know how, when and why people might use your products and services. That gives you an excellent basis for your marketing, because you'll know exactly how you benefit your customers' lives and where (and when) they'll need your stuff.

A whole other collection of questions then becomes easier, such as: Will you build a website or just do everything through social media? What will you write in posts, adverts and other content that potential customers will read? Which social media channels will you use? This might seem like an impossible list of questions for something which might only turn out to be a hobby. They're essential to that side hustle's chances of becoming a viable business though. Unless you know who you're selling to and how, it's impossible to estimate with any degree of accuracy what your costs will be and how much you'll make in your first year. It's so easy to waste money on advertising but if you get it right, you'll hit the jackpot. It took me years to realise that I was selling peace of mind, wonderful experiences and increased sales whenever talking to prospects about their cleaning services. A talent for sales would never have developed during the early 2000's into partnerships with some of the biggest companies in the UK without that lightbulb moment.

You can't make money from a side hustle and build it into a successful business unless you know where your prospects hang-out and what you can give that they can't get or aren't getting from your competitors. Rushing this process will only cost you money.

For example, if 90% of your customers spend hours on Instagram every day, then there's not much use in paying for bus advertising. Pay for much more effective social media adverts instead. Don't just pick the cheapest advertising campaign available because you want to save money. Not reaching a sufficiently high number of potential customers will cost you thousands in lost business over the long-term. Making smart investments of time and money will help you to map out exactly when you can leave your job and become a full-time business owner. Mark the date in the diary and start counting down the days. Why not make today Day 1?

Chasing validation

*M* and I knew exactly how long we'd have to work for to buy Mr Wheatley's franchises outright. I was able to build new relationships with business owners who would benefit from our developing range of services and, very soon afterwards, Mr Wheatley was scrambling to keep the blueprint for *Keen Kleen* under his brand. His solution was to appoint me as his sales lead, giving me a full-time job, a healthy pay rise and a lovely new office. At that point, I was able to finally leave the family business completely and embark on a new journey with Mr Wheatley's business. A much-improved deal followed that came closer to properly valuing my contributions. The franchises I'd worked so hard to buy coming back under his brand was not something that upset me, because I was now free from their debt and was enjoying the benefits of the improved deal. The deals which I had won independently still remained separate though. *M* looked after those.

There aren't many times in life where your side hustle grows so much that it gives you a profitable business and a key role in growing someone else's business at the same time. Focusing on completing every task that lands in your inbox to excellent standards gives you more opportunities all-round. Excellence isn't just limited to big things. Excellence is a lifestyle choice to give everything your best effort, all the time. It's that perseverance and meticulous attention to detail that will power you through difficult times and give you the motivation to develop ambitious plans into lucrative realities.

# One phone call really can change everything…

Nowadays employers might headhunt on LinkedIn. They also might meet you at an event and then try to arrange a *Zoom* call from there. The mid-90s had none of that. I was busy trying to win as many new deals as I possibly could in my new role and changing jobs was the last thing on my mind. While an emerging *Keen Kleen* was employing 40 people, it was more lucrative for me to hand those operations over to *M* and focus on business development for Mr Wheatley, which was the part of the job I most enjoyed. After all, what's the point of working all those hours to improve your lifestyle, if you then miss out on an

## No Problem is Permanent

opportunity to work in a role that you really enjoy. Leading Mr Wheatley's sales team used the best of my growing entrepreneurial skills, while providing me with a much more stable income than self-employment could have offered. He never really treated me as his equal, which hurt, but I was willing to get on with the job because it provided us with much more stability whilst we continued to build *Keen Kleen.*

Then... the phone rang.

"Hello, is that Lloyd Ansermoz?" began the voice on the other end of the line.

"Yes, who's speaking please?" I answered, intrigued. Then I followed it up by asking (optimistically), "Were you looking for any support maintaining your site?"

"Look, I'll cut to the chase," was the direct response that came back down the line, "My name is Peter and I run one of the UK's biggest managed services providers. I'm looking for someone to lead our new Midlands office. That person is you, Lloyd. All the business you've won has got you a lot of attention. Can we arrange another call to discuss terms?"

And there it was...the validation I'd spent so long searching for so long all wrapped up in one phone call. Of the many calls I expected to receive each day, one asking me to change jobs was something so out of the blue and audacious that it could have come from a film script. At the time though, there was no other way for the business to contact me without making the reason for their reaching out completely obvious to Mr Wheatley. The call came from an exciting Warrington-based facilities management firm called *Indepth Managed Services*. Their work up north was well-known and to get a call from them was really quite something. The voice on the other end was the firm's owner, Peter Roach. Not calling him back would just have been daft. His call started a long business relationship in which he would become a mentor to me and would play key roles throughout my career. After quickly agreeing to ring Peter back, I went to the nearest payphone I could find and continued the conversation. Then things got really interesting.

Peter continued:

"Lloyd, we want you and I know you want to join us, the only question left is: how much is this going to cost me? We'd like to offer you a £15k basic salary rising to £30k with bonuses that you'll secure easily. We'll also throw in a luxury company car. You'll build our Midlands operation to £1m+ turnover over the next year and then more opportunities will follow from there. Let's build a great business and make some even better money together."

That was double what my peers earnt (+ the car of course). Better still, Peter had no problem with *M* continuing to service the clients we'd won independently of Mr Wheatley. Most importantly of all, Peter shared my ambition for growth. He was offering me everything I'd ever wanted: the respect of someone who'd already built a thriving business; the chance to build a £1M+ business myself; and a healthy salary which would only increase with time.

There was only one thing I could think to say in response: "When can I start?"

Before too much longer, I informed Mr Wheatley of my intention to leave and went to my new office in West Brom armed with a phone book and a prestigious cleaning contract with *Kays Catalogues*, a pre-internet pioneer of flexible payments. The most important thing I took with me to *Indepth* was the trust of a business owner who truly respected me and was willing to invest in me. Thanks to a shrewd business acquisition by Peter, the Midlands office was developing a business that already serviced *Kays* and a few other big clients rather than starting completely from scratch.

# Never underestimate the value of a great mentor...

Everyone should have a mentor. Even if you're achieving all your goals in life, there's always something that you can learn from a more experienced and successful person. I'll always be grateful to Peter and his wife Jackie for encouraging me to believe that I had the potential to become a business leader in the cleaning industry. Mr Wheatley had always talked down to me and enjoyed making me feel smaller than him. In his eyes, he was a manager and I was just a 'cleaner' with a knack for sales. If you're currently leading a team, please try to be like Peter instead.

If someone comes to you with an idea, highlight the parts that are good so that they can go back, work on them, and improve the bits that weren't so good. Never let your assumptions blind you to someone's potential and lead you to just dismiss them out of hand.

## No Problem is Permanent

There's nothing more demoralising than being told that you'll never amount to anything and that you'll never achieve your goals. Find ways to motivate anyone who you're mentoring so that they seek to improve themselves every day. Peter and Jackie knew that, at the time, I needed recognition of my achievements to feel as though they were valid. They gave me exactly that.

Peter and Jackie's support motivated me to work hard every day and move further up the corporate ladder. I finally felt like I could stay with a business for the long-term and put my all into growing *Indepth*. Having started as a Supervisor on the *Dairy Crest* site only a few years ago, I was now invited to attend *Indepth's* Board meetings and paid a £100 bonus (which went a long way back then) just for turning up to each meeting. *M* kept an early form of *Keen Kleen* ticking over in the meantime.

I doubt that I would ever have developed *Keen Kleen* to a point where we employed almost 300 people, let alone become MD of *Fidelis,* employing well over 400 people, without Peter and Jackie's mentoring. Contrary to popular opinion, perfect mentors don't have to be perfect humans. In fact, their imperfections often give you hugely valuable perspectives on the real world. Mentors who just paint you a picture of your dream world won't prepare you for some of commercial life's toughest challenges. Sometimes, the business world doesn't always exhibit the greatest ethics and you might respond to its challenges by making short-term decisions that don't make the highlight reel of your reflections later in your career. You don't necessarily need to follow your mentor's example in these situations, but you do need to believe in yourself as much as they believe in themselves and learn to stick by whatever decision you make. If you can learn from and avoid their mistakes on the way to success, you'll save yourself a lot of hassle. Everyone makes mistakes. Owning these mistakes and striving to do better in the future is one of the greatest learnings that anyone can take from life.

It's impossible to realise your purpose before deciding what you don't want to become. Only an unvarnished experience of business life can show you what those 'don'ts' look like in HD. That's why hoping to succeed in business without at least one mentor is a ludicrous idea. This person doesn't need to be a superhero, but they do need to be a business person who has experienced the success you're aspiring to (even if by a route you're not 100% sold on). Success leaves clues and you'll never build your own path to success if you can't find those clues.

## Chasing validation

Never feel bad if your time feels like it's taking longer than a bus to come. Take on board as much advice as you can, learn as much as you can and then, eventually, you'll launch a project that nobody else can match.

By the time *Keen Kleen* was finally established in August 2000, formal company incorporation was essential for looking after the dozens of people we employed. Before then though, I needed to learn how to turn a phone book into a business. Looking back to that first day working for *Indepth*, I still couldn't fully picture myself owning a large business outright. I just knew that Peter and Jackie had given me more support professionally than anyone else I'd previously worked for or with. I owed it to them and myself to build as many lucrative, long-term relationships for *Indepth* as possible. Apart from sheer graft, an essential route to this success was to pursue contracted regular work instead of old-fashioned project-based deals. These old-fashioned deals secured large jobs which were great at the time but were then not followed up by further work for many months and were not always paid for enthusiastically by clients. Regular contracted work transforms projects into partnerships. Clients are serviced regularly for at least several years and payments are made regularly over the length of the contract, avoiding unpaid invoices sitting around for months. This approach helped not only to surpass Peter's £1 million turnover target but also enabled *Indepth* to work with some of the best-known and most trusted brands in the UK.

Before all that though, I had some calls to make and a relationship with *Kays Catalogues* to grow...

# Chapter Four

## Growing through flaws

"Let's check-out the catalogue!" was the first thing that my friends and family would say before buying anything new.
 This wasn't just any catalogue. It had the latest fashions, the best toys, and things you never knew you needed around the house – all at sensible prices. Before e-commerce took over the world, *Kays Catalogues* provided a wonderful way for people to buy and enjoy must-have products without breaking the bank. You could pick anything you wanted from one of their catalogues and pay for it over 12 months in instalments. The catalogues were also famous for their artistic front covers which made shoppers' experiences all the more special. No other catalogue carried beautiful drawings of Worcester Cathedral on the cover. That made the catalogues very desirable as collectors' items before people had even browsed the deals inside. Thanks to a sales masterstroke from Peter, the *Kays* team were more than happy for *Indepth* to continue servicing them after Peter's firm inherited the contract from the local company they'd just acquired. It was then on me to grow *Indepth*'s Midlands client-base from there - and quickly. That £1 million first year turnover target never left my mind.

Growing through flaws

After my first day in my new office, the first thing *M* asked me was, "That £1m target Peter mentioned, he's not serious about that, right? There's no way even you can hit that."

"He was!" I replied emphatically, "And I am too. We're doing this. There are no ifs or buts. *Indepth* will have the best offering in the Midlands and nobody will be able to stop us."

I should have added "apart from ourselves" to that last line, but again, Captain Hindsight took another day off with absolutely rubbish timing. Useless!

My weeks at the time looked like 2-3 days at *Indepth*'s head office in Warrington and pretty much the rest of my time working tirelessly out of the brand-new Midlands office in West Bromwich. It was nothing flash, but I had a desk, a phone, a directory and a deck of business cards. That was everything I needed to develop as many relationships with as many different businesses as possible. You have to make your own luck when building a business. Fortunately for me, *Indepth* already serviced one of the region's best-known brands and a few others too, so I wasn't working from a standing start. In a world where perfect starts didn't (and still don't) exist, it was the best I could possibly have hoped for.

# All entrepreneurs are flawed...

Every entrepreneur would love to say that they've always acted in accordance with their values. The reality of business life is far from that though and everyone has flaws. '*Dog kennels*' posed the first moral dilemma I faced from the West Brom office. *Kays Catalogues* regularly received items that were returned or exchanged by customers. That's the reality of any mail-order business. Many of these returned items found their way into storage units that looked exactly like dog kennels and redefined filthy. When I say filthy, I mean completely grim.

Scott, one of the managers at *Kays*, told me, "They're probably worse than the loos, to be fair. We need them cleaned as soon as possible because I can smell them from my office two floors up. Plus, we're running out of space to store newly returned items. Can you help us, Lloyd?"

My answer was, of course, "Absolutely!"

## No Problem is Permanent

Our contract with them then almost doubled in value. This almost provided enough compensation to fix the issue that gnawed away at me over the next few weeks: the *Kays* team were probably paying us twice for the same thing. It seemed impossible that the cleaning of these essential storage units wouldn't have been included in the original contract between the business *Indepth* had just bought and *Kays*. In fact, Peter thought that the service already might have been but couldn't be sure. By the time the issue was raised with me, everyone involved in negotiating that original contract on both sides had moved on in their careers. To make matters even more confusing, nobody from either side could find a copy of the original contract for reference. We probably should have assumed that cleaning the '*dog kennels*' was already included in the original deal and told the *Kays* team that the costs were already covered: but we didn't.

Peter's verdict was, "Lloyd, I've never turned down a profit and don't intend to start today!"

That was that, then.

Looking back now, I wish I had done the right thing. At the time though, I was focused far more on my own goals than the best interests of clients I was working with. Eventually, the issues that were gnawing away at me inspired the culture at the heart of *Fidelis*, where contracts were always precise and clients always came first. Back in the 90's though, the bonuses I was collecting and the validation I was receiving from Peter and Jackie drove me to ignore difficult questions and continue building a future for myself within their business. The deals that *M* was still looking after provided a back-up income if things didn't work out. Safety nets and side hustles had drifted to the back of my mind by then though; I wanted to earn as much as I possibly could and that meant stopping at nothing to hit Peter's £1m turnover target.

Although I was working alone in the West Brom office, I was amazed by the reception I got whenever I visited Peter's Head Office. *Indepth* looked after their team like very few other businesses in the sector. Christmas was particularly special. Everyone either got a whole turkey or a voucher to take home with them for the festive season. Then there was an awesome Christmas party and a tasty lunch too. They got the little things right as well. Water machines that are standard everywhere now were quite rare back then, but they had one at Head Office. Despite some disagreements with management over salary and strategy, the many advantages of staying with *Indepth* at the time meant I just cracked on and got the work done. Sitting still wasn't going to help me to earn more and there was most definitely no shortage of things to do.

Even with the *Kays* name recognition, there was no way that other prestigious deals were about to fall in my lap. I had to do everything in my power to reach as many potential clients as possible. In the pre-internet era this meant spending hours on the phone, trying to drum up work. Many people dislike and even avoid cold calling these days. Entrepreneurs can sometimes waste hours deliberating over how making cold calls might impact their reputations and then stare uncomfortably at their phone for even longer. In that time, they could have made a dozen calls and picked up a lead. Your phone is your friend, and cold calling can work wonders if you do it properly. The most important aspect of any cold call is to respect people's time. Realise that you could be distracting them from an important matter and get to the main benefit of whatever you're selling as quickly as possible. Be polite, introduce yourself quickly and then explain in one sentence or (ideally) less why your product/service would make their lives easier. Many people will hang-up, but some won't. If you ring enough people, you'll sell to at least a few of them. The sales you do make from cold calling could develop into long-term relationships that drive your business forwards. It's definitely worth the effort. Just don't annoy people!

As with most things in life, hard work and confidence shine through here. If you know that you're offering someone an opportunity that will change their life (or in my case, their business) for the better forever, then they need you to call them. Don't hesitate and let someone else phone-up and sell them some rubbish. Believe in what you're selling, make the call, and keep making calls until someone takes advantage of your great offer - just don't over promise during a call. Anything you exaggerate or (worse still) fully make-up will be found out. Then you'll have to deal with livid clients *and* flak from your own team. Save everyone all that trouble and stick to the truth.

Business owners I cold called regularly complimented my straightforward style. A number of them phoned me back several months later and ended up working with us. Although they hadn't needed *Indepth*'s services when I phoned the first time, they appreciated the respect I'd shown them. That seemingly 'unsuccessful' cold call had laid the groundwork for a long-term relationship. The more you put yourself out there in sales, the

## No Problem is Permanent

more you get. It's that simple. If you only put 50% into anything, then you won't get 51% or more out of it. The most successful entrepreneurs I've had the pleasure of sharing time with stopped at nothing to build their businesses. If there are jobs in your business that you're avoiding, get them sorted this week. Delaying only helps your competitors.

It can be immensely difficult to apply this kind of work ethic consistently, particularly when aspects of the company you're generating business for are making you unhappy. At the time, a lot of the unhappiness I was feeling centred around feelings of being underpaid. What had initially seemed like an awesome deal seemed significantly less awesome when I saw how much some of the senior managers up in Warrington were making for doing far less work than me. It would be easy to look back and say that every day I was striving to better-service clients, but back then money in my pay packet and the status it created were on the top of my mind. Whatever you're feeling, sometimes you just have to work through things anyway though. When you have loved ones to support and bills to pay, you just have to get the work done, even if it doesn't make you feel happy and fulfilled.

And so...my work building relationships for *Indepth* didn't stop when I put the phone down. I would also regularly visit businesses around the region and ask the owners if they felt like they were enjoying the cleaning services that they deserved. Very often, they weren't. If I had just sat in the office hoping for the best, some of *Indepth*'s most prestigious projects at the time (and far more of my commission) would have gone elsewhere. Besides, nobody needs a pile of dusty business cards on their desk anyway. Back then, that was a measure of whether you were looking hard enough for sales. If you were on the same batch of cards for months, you hadn't knocked on enough doors. Whatever's driving your desire for success, growth requires relentlessness. You have to want success more than anyone else does. If you're put off by the first hurdle you face, then you'll never reach the second. An advantage of visiting businesses in person is that you make an awesome first impression and instantly show your determination to succeed. More importantly, showing up to someone's site tells them just that - you show up. Particularly in the cleaning industry, so many snappily-dressed salespeople only show up when they absolutely have to and then disappear as soon as they've sold. Business owners far prefer to deal with someone who enjoys being on their site(s) and focuses on helping them to grow before discussing a sale and associated fees. They also want to know that the same person will be on hand to visit them with just as much enthusiasm if something doesn't go according to plan during the project.

At one time (sadly), I resembled one of these salesmen and relished that role far more than I would like to admit. Although I regularly visited sites and checked-in with new and long-term clients, it was obvious to me that our team was overpromising and under delivering. That should have gnawed away at me far more than it did, but I was so focused on selling that I disregarded those concerns completely.

I would put any issues down to "Just being a phase" or would end up promising that "Something will change asap!"

Looking back, that was totally the wrong way to go about things as I was just deflecting blame for some of the problems that came up on a daily basis rather than tackling them head on. That approach was easier and helped me to sell more. Now I know better: no problem is permanent. There's always a solution for everything if you're determined to find it. Refusing to find those solutions just leads to problems dragging on and very often getting worse.

If life were a book of mistakes though, we would all spend so long writing that there would be no time left to build businesses. Later businesses gave me the opportunity to become the person and business owner who I wanted to be rather than the person I needed to be to advance my career all those years ago. One thing that has remained constant throughout my business career is a desire to work harder than anybody else. It's a source of great pride that over the decades, my focus on client happiness and delivering world-class service grew as strong as that work ethic.

Clients notice if you do the extra work that others aren't prepared to even attempt. The thought of you going the extra mile then sticks in their minds when they're making final procurement decisions. Everyone has a choice about who they work with. Taking business for granted is the first step on a slippery slope towards losing clients. Business owners can slide down this slope so easily. All it takes is an assumption that a client will never leave and standards start dropping. Sadly, this is an all too familiar feature of a modern era where certain facilities management providers drop their standards, expecting that clients will find completing the TUPE legal paperwork (relating to the HR aspects of changing suppliers) required to switch to another provider too frustrating to bother with. Businesses are cottoning on to this and they aren't impressed. Frustrating your company's biggest supporters to a point where they only stay with you because of legal small print won't do anything to grow your reputation.

When you're planning your business, focus on how you'll keep these supporters happy. World-class customer service should stay at the forefront of every business owner's mind, all of the time. If you always go above and beyond then you'll always stay one step ahead of your competitors and secure the best work going. That's why we aimed to put world-class customer service at the centre of everything we did at *Keen Kleen* and ultimately achieved that goal with *Fidelis*. It's funny how your greatest career disappointments can quickly transform into your greatest motivations. Without forcing myself to examine the flaws in my business priorities all those years ago, I would never have enjoyed, created and shared so much success through those later businesses. No matter how well you think you're doing in any business situation, never forget to keep learning. Then you'll put yourself in the best possible position to improve and surpass that success in your future ventures.

# But don't forget to look after yourself...

Back in the West Brom office, there was no time for hindsight. My absolute determination to build a fantastic reputation for myself, climb the corporate ladder and increase my salary at *Indepth* meant that I worked harder for them than I'd ever worked in any role previously. The regular travel to Warrington and back took its toll though. When I got the chance to work with Peter again later on in my career, I moved to Warrington full-time and managed operations there. After leaving the situation with Mr Wheatley behind, journey times were the last thing on my mind. I was ready to do whatever it took and travel wherever was needed to secure my financial future. I had already experienced long trips to and from jobs during my time cleaning cellars in Manchester. That didn't make the process any easier though. My experience just meant that I was fully prepared to make the sacrifices needed to generate as much business as possible for *Indepth*. All business owners realise that sacrifices are an unavoidable part of the job.

## Growing through flaws

When you get further on in your career you have more options, but these much less glamorous parts of the job are often unavoidable when you're younger.

There are so many other memories I could have made in the time I spent driving up and down the motorway.

*M* would often call me while I was travelling and ask, "Why do you have to go on all these trips? We want you here."

I would reply, "I have to do this. This is the best way for us to build the lives we want."

Success is often a lonely process and sometimes even those closest to you won't fully understand your drive. You don't worry about things like that when you're young though. You just seize opportunities and pursue them to the max. Your focus is on building a better tomorrow, even if today (and yesterday) fell well below your expectations on the wellbeing front.

Sadly, for me, all that travel may well have contributed to the health battles I fought through later in life. I would urge all entrepreneurs to consider your health when building your businesses. Your own health may seem like the last thing on your mind when you're busy working, but it's the most important aspect of life. Entrepreneurs nowadays have so many more options than I had back then to improve their work-life balance. In the modern era of virtual meetings, it's possible to keep track of projects and liaise with colleagues without having to be in the office or on site in-person all the time. Use the flexibility that this technology provides to reduce those tiring journeys and spend more time with your loved ones. Save longer journeys for the times when it really counts (like crucial sales meetings and site visits) so that you're not spending huge chunks of your week in the car or on trains. Many clients and colleagues are happy to catch-up on calls. If that works for them, then let it work for you too. One of the most important aspects of growing a business is to use your time productively. Focus on how much you're getting done and how much you're selling rather than how long you're spending doing things that aren't actually boosting your profits.

No Problem is Permanent

# Keep teams connected to maintain excellent standards long-distance...

As more and more businesses throughout the Midlands and elsewhere trusted us with their maintenance requirements, *Indepth's* Head Office in Warrington became more and more distant from day-to-day operations. While this didn't present any substantial issues initially, eventually, Head Office began to lose crucial influence over operations across regional clients' sites. The only updates they had on the quality of work across these sites came from a phone call every few days from one of those old-fashioned phones with the dials that you spun in the site offices. Anyone could say anything over that phone and there was no guarantee that accurate data was making its way back to Warrington at any level of speed.

"Yes, yes, everything's fine boss, nothing to worry about here," was a response that often arrived at Board meetings from sites which seemed to generate more client complaints than revenue.

Despite a growing awareness of challenges faced across these sites, there seemed to be less and less that anyone in Head Office could do to fix them.

Changes in senior leadership at *Indepth* only increased the focus on Warrington and widened Head Office's separation from day-to-day activities even more. While regional teams could manage this distance to some extent, the number of sites we were managing made it difficult to bring the wider team together under the same company culture. Different teams made a variety of decisions, and sadly, some of those decisions fell short of both our and our clients' expectations. Newer team members across the country were disconnected from the core team which had made *Indepth* so successful and every day was becoming an uphill struggle. Things got so bad that Warrington had to set up an unofficial complaints department to manage all of the negative feedback that was overwhelming the main phone line. It's such a shame that the human side of company culture that the firm got so right wasn't matched by the customer service levels delivered by those who *Indepth* trusted to represent their brand nationally.

Growing through flaws

The importance of a well-rounded company culture (including world-class customer service) in binding teams together cannot be overstated. Many years later with *Fidelis*, the customer service training that all our people received meant that they were always a cheery and helpful presence around sites. If someone walked past them, our operatives would smile and say "Hello!"

If someone was lost, they would point them in the right direction. Although these are minor gestures, they can make a huge difference to a client's day. Imagine you're having a horrible day, and a friendly face lets you know that things are never as bad as they seem. Would you go back to your desk feeling happier and with a renewed sense of purpose? Of course you would! Would you then recommend that provider if management asked for your input when the contract came up for review? You'd probably do that too.

The same goes for senior managers and directors who visit clients' sites. At *Fidelis*, if I was on the way to a meeting and passed a site we serviced en route, I would always drop in and say "Hello!" As well as reassuring operatives that I appreciated their efforts, this also allowed me to sense the mood on site and be on hand if anyone wanted a quick chat. You want to make an effort to speak to as many operatives as possible and make them feel as though you share their passion and appreciate their hard work. You also want to show clients how determined you are to deliver as much value for them as possible. These visits conveniently offer great opportunities to upsell too but doing it in the right way matters hugely.

Some people will visit and spend the time trying to flog extra services without thinking about whether their clients actually need them (like I did with those '*dog kennels*'). The much better way to upsell is to take a keen interest in what's happening on site. If you notice a problem with flooring, you can raise the issue in a way which secures you some more work, but more importantly, saves the client from a more serious problem which could have endangered their teams if left unspotted. Make every sale you agree one that helps clients to achieve their own goals and boost their productivity. Focusing solely on boosting your own order book when selling tends to come back to haunt you at some point, even if that point comes long into the future. Remember people's names too. They won't forget you if you don't forget them. Not everything is rocket science! Sometimes just being a positive

No Problem is Permanent

presence on site can save you from several hours of crisis meetings later on.

Sadly, I didn't embrace this client-centred approach to site visits back in the 90s. Strains between businesses I was looking after for *Indepth* and senior management in Warrington around poor-quality work deteriorated into serious crises and eventually, contract cancellations. The wide range of apps available nowadays could have delayed or even reversed this deterioration significantly by bringing sites around the country closer together. From sharing advice to just connecting and chatting, this technology can give an operative in Birmingham the chance to get to know a colleague in Warrington even if they've never met each other in-person.

Moreover, these apps show clients exactly how many hours operatives have worked on agreed projects. This fosters a culture of openness and transparency which significantly reduces the risk of quality varying between sites. Real-time updates allow action to fix any issues to be taken as quickly as possible. There's no need to get on a site phone to let Head Office know about an issue. They'll find out beforehand and call you to work through potential solutions to present to the client. Anticipating this and calling them first is always a great plan. Then you and someone from Head Office can sit-down with them for an in-person meeting to sort things out. Sadly, none of that technology was available all those years ago.

It's also hugely difficult to meet clients in-person and arrange hospitality when your company directors work three hours away from your clients (in good traffic). Clients like to meet with directors and the further away those directors live and work, the more challenging those meetings are to organise. Moreover, hospitality has to have a local meaning to be effective. The *Aston Villa FC* season tickets that our family business had bought for the *Dairy Crest* team worked because our team and theirs were all lifelong *Villa* supporters. That wouldn't have worked if our business had been based miles further North and our team had all supported *Liverpool FC*. It would have been immediately obvious to Midlands-based businesses that we didn't share their passion for the *Villa* and the whole thing would have fallen flat. A mixture of data, local knowledge and availability of senior staff transforms long-distance business relationships into premium local services. These difficulties and my own inexperience at the time made it near impossible for me to replicate the relationships I'd built with *Dairy Crest*'s top team with *Indepth*'s clients.

I hoped that winning a prestigious contract with a huge multinational law firm (worth £160k a year) for *Indepth* would help to turn things around. Despite an initially strong relationship, the law firm had grown unhappy with the quality of work delivered by certain members of *Indepth*'s wider regional team. The size of the contract (14 operatives cleaning one site per night) had led *Indepth* to outsource the work to another provider to seal the deal, because they didn't have that kind of capacity in-house at the time.

Outsourcing is normal in the cleaning industry. It happens most often when one provider secures agreements to work on more sites than their own people can cover. Therefore, they hire another company to represent them in front of clients and clean these sites. Outsourcing can carry great reputational risk as another business may not share the same values as yours. When values differ, standards begin to differ too. Clients can then become dissatisfied with poor quality work. All the backlash then comes back to your business, who the company you've outsourced to has represented so poorly. At *Fidelis*, we avoided this risk by refusing to outsource any contracted cleaning services. We always brought operatives working on even our most distant sites fully into our team. They all received the same training that our core teams enjoyed, so that everyone was on the same page and knew how highly we valued and appreciated them. Standards across all sites then very often improved.

Unfortunately, as with others regionally, the agency that *Indepth* had outsourced the law firm's contract to were nowhere near as diligent as Peter and tolerated poor standards. They made the challenges my colleagues at the time based elsewhere in the country were facing look like mild Monday morning inconveniences. The service that the law firm received continued to decline and, as much as we tried, there was no way that they would stay with *Indepth*. I was watching the biggest contract I had negotiated with a client so far disintegrate before my eyes. However, a conversation with the law firm indicated that they retained trust in me and would be more than happy for a different team to complete the work under my supervision.

Their Head of Facilities Management, Rob, phoned me and said, "Look, Lloyd, we think that you're an outstanding professional, but to describe your team as 'looking after' our site

## No Problem is Permanent

is going it a bit. We're starting to get complaints from staff about the cleanliness of our main office and before too long, clients will start noticing, if they haven't already. Either you get a new team or we find a new provider. That's it unfortunately. As much as I like and respect you as a professional, I can't keep justifying these mediocre standards to my bosses. I can actually see stains on my office carpet as I'm calling you now."

The possibility of losing the biggest account I'd ever won was not something I was willing to contemplate, and fortunately, *M* was still managing what would become our first accounts as *Keen Kleen Ltd*. A change of providers to *Keen Kleen* was possible and could be done without the law firm experiencing any inconvenience. The opportunity to change some of the things I hadn't liked in my current role and test out some of my ideas with such a prestigious client was too good to turn down. A decision was made and my business career was never the same again.

I left *Indepth*, formally incorporated *Keen Kleen* as a business and the law firm became one of our most prestigious and regular clients. *Keen Kleen* was a first step on the road to building successful businesses through my own ideas about company culture. The opportunity to add the law firm into *Keen Kleen*'s client portfolio began a series of successful tender wins for my old side-hustle which then became a sizeable business. 7 years later *Keen Kleen* was enjoying multi-million pound annual turnover. Yet two years after that landmark achievement, a severe cash flow crisis left us in major difficulties. I couldn't think of a way out of the situation other than selling the business.

The phone rang again with perfect timing: it was Peter...

## Never burn your bridges...

Peter called me from his home in Majorca. We had an excellent conversation about everything that had followed my discussions with the law firm and smoothed a lot over. No business career is regret-free. There are always: things you wished you could change: things you wish you hadn't said; and things that you wish had panned out differently.

After a few more calls and meetings, he realised the financial situation I was in and said, "Lloyd, I'm happy to buy up *Keen Kleen*'s contracts but on one condition: you come back to *Indepth*. Nobody sells like you. You were always great at that."

Growing through flaws

So, in 2007, I came back to *Indepth*. My ambition was to extend my role beyond selling by implementing new ideas around culture capable of driving the growth that was stalling when I left. While some of these ideas had inspired *Keen Kleen*'s peak, their implementation back then hadn't delivered long-term growth that created generational personal and financial wealth for everyone involved with *Keen Kleen*. If the team I was rejoining at *Indepth* could just put everything together and retain clients long-term, we could deliver amazing results that the industry had never seen before. My hopes were that everything I had learned over the previous decades and successfully demonstrated during *Keen Kleen*'s early years, combined with what Peter had continued building in my absence, would be more than enough to get us over the line.

Giving each director of *Indepth* a copy of one of the most inspiring business culture books I've ever read, Dr Paddi Lund's *Building the Happiness-Centred Business*, seemed like a great way to promote new thinking about company culture. I still struggle to process how badly this suggestion was taken.

Picture the scene. I walked into a director's office, let's call him 'Geoff'. "Geoff, here's a really important book about business culture. It means a lot to me and I hope it can inspire you too," I said hopefully.

Then his response came. The wisdom inside this book came flying back at me...literally. In fact, all 148-pages hit me square in the chest. My heart then dropped in the few seconds I had to brace for Geoff's somehow even more disrespectful verbal response.

"Hahahahahahahahaha…" he crowed, "why would I read **THAT RUBBISH???**"

I've never left a professional encounter of any kind feeling so hurt and deflated. Nonetheless, I kept trying to promote positive change at *Indepth*. After moving my family up to Warrington, I wasn't going to come straight back to the Midlands. These efforts often went ignored though.

Worse still, some of the great things I'd remembered from all those years ago had either stopped or changed beyond recognition. The Christmas turkey had been scrapped and replaced with nothing. The Christmas lunch became six mince pies (shared between six of us). When asking where the water machine had gone, I was shown the tap. It was clear that they only ever saw me as a sales guy and didn't appreciate my efforts to influence other areas of the business at all. Eventually, it became impossible to stay and after some negotiation, two years later, I left again.

I could clearly see that a world-class company culture, supported by innovative use of data was key to sustaining long-term client relationships and boosting profitability. But *Indepth* was formed in 1978 and their way of doing things had proved successful over many years. If I believed that a different approach could generate even more success, I had to go out and prove myself (again). I probably should have shown a greater appreciation for their past when suggesting new ideas, but sometimes you get so passionate about certain changes that they become all you ever think and talk about.

Even if you think you know it all, you don't. It can take decades to finally see your dreams manifest into reality. I sold *Fidelis* in 2021. That's 10 years after leaving *Indepth* (again); 21 years after setting up *Keen Kleen*; 27 years after first meeting Peter; and almost 30 years after those crucial early experiences alongside the *Dairy Crest* team. Life as a business owner is a long journey with far more flaws than you could ever have imagined when excitedly filling out your company registration forms. It's up to you to see the valuable lessons in those flaws and grow through them by making better decisions in future. Each stage of my career taught me lessons that made the next stage happier and more profitable. Through everything, Peter and I always retained respect for each other.

Never forget that great businesses don't exist without excellent professional relationships and patience either. Significant supplies of both of those qualities won't see you far wrong…

# Chapter Five

## Success is never a solo act

There are several times in my life where I've felt more nervous than I can put into words. Long before the success of *Fidelis*, one of those moments came as I was queueing at the bank after leaving *Indepth* for the first time. Everything was in place for my newly incorporated business, *Keen Kleen* to take-off apart from one thing: cash. Financing the projects we'd won would take £10,000 we didn't have. So, like almost all business owners at the time, I found myself waiting to speak to a bank manager and hoping that they would support my vision. The first meeting didn't go well at all.

"There's absolutely no way that we'd lend that kind of money to a startup with no proven track-record!" was the incredibly rude response I got for my efforts from a local bank manager - let's call him 'Mr Unhelpful'.

The problem was that I had a track-record, but it was largely reflected in cash salaries which I'd already spent. Fortunately, those salaries had enabled me to build a Sutton Coldfield house which had seen better days into an excellent family home. Howard Crow, who was one of the best bank managers I ever had the privilege of meeting, could see from my previous earnings and house purchasing history that I knew what it took to be successful in business. He put these together to secure me the finance I urgently needed exceptionally quickly.

## Businesses need great bank managers...

My first meeting with Howard was fantastic. He was imaginative and genuinely supportive of my ideas. He invited me to apply for a loan and his response when we met again took imaginative problem-solving to new levels.

"Thanks so much for your impressive application, Lloyd," he said in a warm voice I'll never forget.

"As you know we can't provide you with a business loan for £10,000 as you don't have a long-history of business ownership...however [one of those promising 'howevers'], I've noticed that you recently purchased a charming property just down the road from here, is that right?"

I wasn't quite sure what to say in response. "Well, yes, thank you. we're doing it up!" seemed like a good place to start.

"I bet the kitchen refurbishment is quite pricey," Howard continued, "How about we loan you £10,000 to renovate your kitchen? I'm sure that you'd love one of those snazzy new cookers."

After not disguising my surprise at Howard's suggestion particularly well, I said, "Howard, I need a business loan - not a new cooker. I hardly spend any time at home anyway".

He sat back in his chair and smiled. "I know Lloyd, I'm sorry to inform you that our bank's policies won't let me give a loan of that size to a new business, but we would be delighted to offer you a £10,000 loan for kitchen refurbishments, secured against your mortgage. I can see from your income that you would easily repay our loan in good time. Besides...by that time you'll be able to show us your business growth figures and can apply separately for any business finance that you might need."

Then the penny, or rather, the million pennies dropped. I gladly accepted the bank's loan for refurbing my kitchen. Not much cooking went on though.

That didn't matter as I was able to build a far nicer kitchen many years later after selling *Fidelis*. The loan was pivotal in

## Success is never a solo act

turning *Keen Kleen* from a profitable side-hustle to a thriving business. The £10,000 meant that we could provide the law firm who had followed me to my new business with the services they needed and then grow and grow from there. I will always be grateful to Howard for believing in me all those years ago. Without his trust and support, I would have been absolutely stranded after leaving *Indepth*. Successful entrepreneurs are often quick to celebrate their own accomplishments but quite a bit slower to give credit where it's due and thank those whose partnership they depended on in the early days. Whenever any professional takes on a client, they always take on some level of risk. If I had squandered thousands of pounds on trendy hobs and left Howard with a hole in his books, he might have lost his job. That's one of the reasons why I was determined to repay his trust with a business large enough to maintain a regular credit facility directly with his bank. While businesses don't need loads and loads of partners, every entrepreneur needs to be able to trust a select circle of individuals with expertise in key areas.

Banking is one of them. Business planning is another. Before formally incorporating *Keen Kleen*, I'd never put a business plan together before. My focus had always been on building relationships and selling. The admin side of business life had always been handled by other people. So long as my wages arrived in my account every month, I didn't really give how they got there a second thought. Every business owner would like to pay their monthly wage bill from a portion of their revenues with a fair chunk left over, but sometimes life just doesn't work out like that. Those wages are often paid for through loans secured by business plans. If you can't present a professional business plan, then even the kindest of bank managers will struggle to provide you with the cash needed to keep everything ticking regardless of ups and downs in your sales numbers.

## You never stop learning...

Luckily enough for me, I knew Chris Barrow. Chris is probably one of the most influential people I've met over the course of my business career. He helped me to organise my sales mind into a business-building mentality. I still remember one of our first sessions vividly.

"Lloyd...I've seen people with busy calendars...but this is something else. How do you get anything done with all the time

## No Problem is Permanent

you spend in meetings? Are they really all necessary?" was Chris' immediate and rather perturbed response after I showed him my diary for the first time.

At the time, I would make the time to meet anyone if I thought they might be able to help with the business. I was getting involved in every aspect of the business too, from sales to picking out the office wallpaper. "I just want to do everything I can to help the business grow," I replied quite defensively while grudgingly accepting that Chris had a point.

"I completely get that, but other people can do most of those jobs. That frees up your time to focus on what you do. More importantly, it also gives your colleagues the freedom to get on with their jobs without worrying about you constantly looking over their shoulders," added Chris.

I'd always thought of diary management as a purely personal thing. Why would my schedule have an impact on the business beyond myself and the people I was meeting? Chris showed me that fixing my diary into shape was the first step to building a more effective and productive team. My ambitions to turn *Keen Kleen* into a multi-million pound business would take a significant knock if I tried to do absolutely everything within the business myself. We all have our weaknesses and if we don't accept them, then those personal weaknesses end up damaging the business as a whole. Taking that step back and realising that I didn't need to sit through every meeting to guarantee successful outcomes gave us a better team and a much healthier growth trajectory. I hammered out with Chris a list of things that I would (and crucially, wouldn't) intervene in and never looked back.

That wasn't the only area that Chris helped me with though. Apart from showing me how to put a business plan together, he encouraged me not to sell to everyone, but to find ideal clients and sell to them instead.

Chris telling me: "Look, you only have so many hours in the day and you want to make sure you're generating as much revenue as possible from every hour you spend working. You just don't have the scale to service small accounts who always want discounts and are never going to grow into larger sites for you to maintain. You want to focus on the larger businesses with multiple sites that need regular maintenance-" was truly a lightbulb moment.

I'd been building client relationships through long-term contracts for some time. Some of them were rather less lucrative

## Success is never a solo act

than I'd initially hoped though, as clients weren't needing additional services. We were stuck at fixed-rate deals that didn't reflect inflation for years at a time. Chris' advice helped me to target clients with regular and evolving needs, so that as our partnerships grew my order book did too. This expanded ideas which had led to success earlier in my business career through managing key relationships with the teams at *Dairy Crest* and *Kays Catalogues* into strategies that I could apply across the whole of my new business.

Huge growth followed at *Keen Kleen* and in my personal life too. Another of my most memorable conversations with Chris turned to books.

"What are you reading, Lloyd?" was a question that used not to get much of a response.

"I don't really have time," was my stock answer.

That conversation marked a turning point though. Chris recommended two books that changed my life. One was *Rich Dad Poor Dad* by Robert. T. Kiyosaki and Sharon Lechter. I read that from cover to cover in a week on a deckchair in Corfu and was so engrossed in it that I hardly saw any of the island. The book has sold well over 30 million copies for a reason and covers different approaches to wealth. It's possible to work all the time and never see the benefits of your hard graft pay off. That was the experience of many families in our neighbourhood when I was growing up. Despite relentless hard work, people often ended up owning very little. They didn't own their own businesses, they didn't have investments and the stock market was something they might occasionally read about in the papers I delivered. This wonderful book emphasises the importance of not just entrepreneurship, but of investing your money and transforming working into asset ownership. Better still, it movingly contrasts the life advice that 'rich dads' and 'poor dads' give their kids about the working world. This gave me some eye-opening and piercingly real examples of where I thought that I'd been earning a huge amount, but I was actually losing huge value and damaging my long-term wealth prospects. While that book changed my approach to money, Chris' other recommendation brought the ideas I was already having about innovating company culture to life.

That second recommendation was Dr Paddi Lund's *Building The Happiness-Centred Business*, the book which would cause unprecedented consternation in Warrington a few years down the line. Paddi was an Australian dentist who Chris knew personally, as his first coaching clients were dentists looking to grow their businesses. Paddi's book gave me inspirational insights into building a business in which: my colleagues were happy because they felt valued and appreciated every day; my clients were happy because they received world-class services; my suppliers were happy because they were treated with respect; and I was happy because my business was generating healthy profits.

Before meeting Chris I had always seen work as just, well - work. The thought of using my time outside of work to consider my purpose in life was something that I never had thought would be useful at all. Reading for self-development turned out to be what transformed me from a talented entrepreneur to a successful business owner. Delving into a book takes you out of your own situation and helps you to view your business from a completely different angle. How would you feel if you were newly hired by your business? Would you feel welcomed by a warm atmosphere? Would you immediately resonate with a company culture that reflected your values? What about if you were one of your prospects weighing up different options? Would you work with your own business?

When you're in the moment, it can be so easy to become so busy that you forget to take a step back. Books give you the space, the thinking time and the new ideas needed to challenge yourself throughout your business journey. Nothing is ever flawless and there are always things to learn and improve on. My partnership with Chris taught me that working on myself would be just as important to *Keen Kleen*'s growth as the work that I was doing behind my desk every day.

## Spread the wealth around...

I never would have met Chris without the help of Noel Farrelly. Long before I'd started working with Chris on a 1:1 basis, Noel urged me to book on to his *Young Entrepreneur* course. The course looked fantastic, but it cost £1900. That was a huge amount back then and there was no way I could have afforded to pay the whole thing in one go. Thankfully for me, Noel was great mates with Chris and persuaded him to allow me to pay for the course in instalments. One of Noel's biggest skills was seeing the potential in people. He was all about building: building wealth, building teams and building entrepreneurs' self-confidence. He could see

## Success is never a solo act

that I was on the road to substantial business success, and assured Chris that I was someone who he would always regret not working with if he didn't give me a place on his highly competitive course. Sometimes you need a partner to fight your corner and persuade one of their friends to give you a chance.

That introduction was only one example of Noel helping me out like that. In his work as a financial planner, he became my version of Kiyosaki and Lechter's *Rich Dad*. While I was often caught in the moment, I felt as though Noel almost had a crystal ball. He would ask me what kind of life I wanted in 30 years' time, where I wanted to live, what pension provision I'd made and when I wanted to retire (an idea I'm still not completely comfortable with). This completely changed my thinking about business. The difference between working out of passion rather than because I needed the money had never crossed my mind. The option that wealth gives you to enjoy the fulfilment of doing something *purely* because you love it is such a liberating experience.

They don't call it 'financial freedom' for nothing. As much as people talk about travel abroad as a moment where they find themselves, you won't get very far if you can't also find money for flights and accommodation too. Not having the worry of constant bills lingering at the back of your mind and weighing you down gives you the chance to spend your time doing things you love. For some people, financial freedom might look like spending a month on the beach in Jamaica or sampling Italy's best pasta. I was lucky enough to spend last August doing both with my wonderful family. If I hadn't met Noel, there's no way I ever would have gone on holidays like that outside of my dreams. I would still have been that star salesman who spent all his money on flashy things and put nowhere near enough of it away for future family beach days.

It was horrible watching my Dad force himself to go to work, even though he was way too ill to be labouring in the bakery, because our family needed the money. I always wanted to be in a position where I could step back from work (while not retiring) and enjoy quality time with my family while my health was still in relatively good nick. Noel mapped out clear strategies that would help me to secure my financial future and do just that.

One day he asked me, "Lloyd, how hard is your money working for you?"

"It's sitting in the bank quite nicely and I've invested the rest, so not too badly," I replied.

## No Problem is Permanent

Noel then paused, smiled and said, "I think we can get it to put an extra shift in for you."

Then, he explained compound interest. If you've got a savings account that increases by 4% every year and you don't touch it for two years, you'll enjoy an 8% increase during that time. That's the compounding magic of earning interest on interest. Too many people only see interest as a negative. It often appears as an extra bill on top of a bill that they already struggled to afford. They don't realise that interest can work for you, if you save your money in the right accounts and pension plans.

This was just one of the hugely valuable life lessons that Noel taught me. Another was that the best way to expand my income was to expand my network.

I actually met Noel at the first networking event I ever attended, after receiving a lovely letter from Howard. It read:

*"Dear Lloyd,*

*I hope that your kitchen refurbishments are going well. If you can spare the time, a group of my most trusted business contacts meets every week to share knowledge and try to help each other to grow. We meet at Aston Wood Golf Club every Tuesday at 7am sharp. You'll make so many great contacts and, most importantly, lifelong friends there. Let me know if you can make it.*

*Yours Sincerely,*

*Howard"*

This group was the first ever *BNI* group in the UK outside of London. *BNI* was taking the world by storm having launched in LA nearly two decades earlier to amazing success. The concept behind the group was truly game-changing and the UK business scene had never seen anything like it before. Instead of people sitting around chatting and hoping to sell their stuff, the *BNI* model was based on the idea that 'givers gain. All members were required to spend the week in between meetings having detailed 1:1 sessions with other members where they would learn about their businesses. It was then your job as a member to find potential leads for these other businesses. In return, they did the same for you. Instead of having just myself, *M* and our small team looking for *Keen Kleen's* next clients, BNI offered me 50 experienced professionals doing everything they could to find me excellent new clients. I joined after the first meeting and quickly afterwards, met Howard and Noel's friends Mark Panayides and Dave Bayliss (Mark's business partner). They knew pretty much everyone who was running a successful business in Birmingham. They had also partnered on some great businesses themselves, starting in printing and ending up with a full-service marketing agency. Through Mark and Dave, I met many clients, suppliers, trusted contacts and friends.

Selfless isn't the word. Despite their own relentlessly busy schedules, they went out of their way to help me to grow my network in a way that delivered sustained business growth too. They also impressed me for two other reasons. Firstly, like Noel, they had massive houses in some of the plushest areas of Birmingham like Four Oaks. Those leafy, gated roads were a different planet from the dusty cobbled streets and back-to-backs I'd grown up around.

What impressed me even more was that they had built these lifestyles for themselves while creating high-quality careers for others. Mark, Dave and Noel were the antithesis of the overbearing managers that I'd struggled to deal with for so long. They understood that they wouldn't have any of their wealth without the wonderful people they employed and all three of them had an approach to business that was streets ahead of others at the time. I wanted to learn as much from them as I possibly could.

# Changing my friends changed my future...

It's said that you become the five people who you spend the most time with. After my marriage to Tracey ended, I spent all my time in the pub. There I met people interested in drinking, fighting, smoking and playing snooker (possibly all at once). I then focused on drinking as much as possible and staying in a semi-permanent state of aggression in case someone annoyed me in any way at all. This was how our group in the pub processed a world that we felt was set against us back then: bouts of rage mixed into even deeper bouts of depression. At the time, my pub friends seemed to offer the best way out of the hurt I was feeling as the world I was building with Tracey collapsed around me. To my immense

## No Problem is Permanent

personal cost, I would fairly quickly realise that I needed new friends, and that hanging out with them just left me deeper in the mire. By contrast, my partnerships with Howard, Chris, Noel, Mark and Dave took me to heights that I never would have imagined reaching when I was at my lowest all those years ago in the pub. Your network truly is your net worth.

As I have gained more and more business experience, I've found that my network has grown alongside me. That young entrepreneur who once struggled to pay a £1900 coaching course fee now gets calls from the owners of businesses sustaining 8-figure turnovers who are looking to sell and move into the next chapter of their lives. They trust me to find maximum value in their businesses and also to refer them to expert advisers, such as lawyers, who can help them to navigate this life-changing process. This is another example of my growing business network - that I only realised was worth building after reading Howard's letter - paying dividends many years later. So many people make the mistake of attending events, trying to add absolutely everybody within sight on *LinkedIn* and then hoping for the best. They're only interested in selling to other attendees and they see networking to learn from people who have walked the path they're on and build long-term partnerships with them as a waste of time. That's exactly why they often come away from these events without long-term partnerships and complaining that networking "Hasn't worked" for them.

Building trust takes time. It would be hugely reckless of me or frankly anyone else to meet someone once at an event and then involve them in a business sale.

Long-term partnerships are about far more than generating sales and sharing introductions. To this day, I always look to learn from people who have got to where I want to be in life. Assuming that you know everything is probably the quickest way to gain nothing from professional relationships and may even cause you to lose quite a bit too. Every event you attend and every new person you meet offer exciting opportunities for personal growth. I remember meeting Noel for the first time and thinking that I didn't need his help because I already understood money. After chatting to him for less than an hour over coffee, I suddenly realised just how many aspects of money's inner-workings I'd never even considered, let alone understood.

Success is never a solo act. You need to constantly seek advice from partners outside of your immediate team, as well as your colleagues, in order to get every task in your business done to a world-class standard without any exceptions. You've probably come across the different ideas of working 'in' your business rather than 'on' your business. Working 'in' your business involves operational tasks like accounts, compliance, marketing, HR, recruitment, keeping clients happy and managing your sales pipeline. Working 'on' your business is the more strategic bit. This work focuses on your growth plans for the business, your overall strategy, your company culture and creating proposals for long-term partnerships with high-profile clients. There's absolutely no point in you spending hours working on legal issues if you've never studied law and you'd much rather be out visiting potential clients. Pay for quality advice instead and hire a trusted lawyer to do what they're great at.

When you start employing dozens and then hundreds of people (and hire experts to help them in specialist areas), you have to step back and appreciate that you've grown from being a business engine to a vital cog in a much larger organisation. My trusted network played a key role in helping me to withdraw from managing day-to-day operations of businesses that I'd invested so much blood, sweat and tears into as *Keen Kleen* and, many years later, *Fidelis* grew. These friends had experienced the same process which made it much easier to cope with the natural emotions that come from trusting others to run your business for you. What could have felt like a sudden change became a natural progression along the winding (and continuing) road of my business journey. That progress continues to this day. After every achievement, I always ask myself,

"What's next?"

Don't ever settle.

Always drive yourself to achieve, learn and earn more from each step of your business journey.

Like most journeys, yours will have at least a few drop-off points too. After the first time I left *Indepth*, there was a colossal amount that I needed to work on within myself in order to transform *Keen Kleen* into the success it became. Even then, I wouldn't have said that I was completely happy with my life. Like everyone, there comes a point in every day where I'm alone with my own thoughts. Those thoughts haven't always given me the confidence to speak in front of huge audiences or be the business owner that I need to be at key moments of my journey. You can have all the support in the world, but if you don't have incredible self-belief, you'll struggle to progress through your goals. Thankfully, things are much better now. Back when I was transforming *Keen Kleen* from a side-hustle to a successful business though, I had to jump through hurdles in my mind as well as business hurdles to grow personally and professionally...

# Chapter Six

## Shifting barriers

It was a wonderful evening. All six of us were sitting together on the same table enjoying a sumptuous dinner. I still remember the pudding: a warm, crumbly chocolate cake with sauce that just melted as soon as it touched my mouth. Then came an announcement that I'd never imagined hearing when drowning my sorrows in the pub all those years ago:

"And the winner of Best New Business of the Year is...*Keen Kleen*!"

We had just won a top regional newspaper's highest award for a startup. I nearly dropped my cake down my tux. Pete Windsor, who would later become one of our managers, jumped up and down and made so much noise that he almost made the front page himself. A booming "Yesss, get innn!!! Olé, olé, olé, olé!" filled the banqueting suite so loudly that a few people living down the road from the venue would have heard Pete celebrating too. I hope they were as happy as we were.

"It's wonderful to see such passion from our winners. That was quite a reaction!" said the kind MC presenting us with our award in *the* politest mildly concerned voice he could muster.

No Problem is Permanent

Thankfully, nobody noticed the cake down my tux after that.

It was the first time I'd ever worn a tux and the moment was just so special. My first tux fit perfectly and showed just how far I'd come in beautifully soft velvet. The awards dinner and our win didn't just recognise the amazing first year of business *Keen Kleen* had enjoyed since its formal incorporation. The dinner and most importantly, the win, validated all those hours I'd spent cleaning cellars and, later, industrial sites at 1am. It also validated my growth from becoming an operative to a franchisee to a business owner. Winning such a prestigious award was absolutely massive for *Keen Kleen*.

Then the next year, things got even better. We only went and won *Business of the Year*. After only two years of trading, we beat businesses which had been established for over a decade to the prize. Enquiries from huge companies around the country followed. Before the phones started ringing the next day though, I was just taking it all in, sitting in *Aston Villa*'s Holte Suite. I couldn't help thinking about those Villa season tickets that the family business had bought for the *Dairy Crest* managers. A journey that had started in the stands had now included two fantastic moments in my favourite club's prestigious hospitality suite. One of my first VIP experiences of a *Villa* match featured here too as Pete not only outdid his celebrations from the previous year, but made a statement in the auction as the evening drew to a close. I had given Pete a budget of £500 to bid. After briefly glancing at me, he jumped up again and shouted "£500!!" when the evening's auctioneer invited bids for a luxury matchday experience at *Villa*'s next home game. The bid was successful and Pete was ecstatic. I was less impressed.

"We could have got that for less than £300, what are you doing bidding our whole budget for the auction as your first bid for lot 1?" I asked. Pete's response taught me something more valuable than any saving could have done.

"That's not the point though, Lloyd, is it? We've had a fantastic night and all the money's going to charity."

From that moment on I always made sure to bid over the odds in charity auctions, just because it's the right thing to do.

# Let great leaders accomplish what you can't...

Shifting barriers

Back in 2000, starting a business seemed like a massive jump. The goal was just to survive and winning an award wasn't something I'd even thought possible. Like most entrepreneurs, the first hurdles I had to jump over were the ones in my own mind; the ones that said, "No, that's too risky" or asked, "Are you sure you can cope with that?" whenever a new business idea came to mind.

The best response to these thoughts is just pure honesty. Maybe you can't accomplish certain things on your own, but with the right team, you can accomplish anything. The £3.7 million annual turnover that *Keen Kleen* generated at its peak would never have been possible without the contributions of each of the 230 people who made our wider team so special before the business was sold in 2007. Experts outside of the business played a crucial role in that growth too. Developing the relationships which I'd started to build with them when formally setting up *Keen Kleen* into long-term partnerships absolutely underpinned the success that followed.

The decision to formally incorporate *Keen Kleen* only came about because of a casual chat with my lawyer friend, Steve Broomhall.

When discussing my then side-hustle with me, Steve asked, "I'm loving your growth Lloyd, how many people are you currently employing?"

"Oh, about 40," was my understated but immensely proud reply.

Then Steve shocked me. "If any of them sue you, as things stand, they can come after you personally."

That risk had never crossed my mind as all the relationships I'd built until then were based on trust. Surely, nobody would try to put a claim in just to try to damage me and get some money?

"You'd hope that never happens. All business owners do!" Steve continued. "But law isn't about hoping, it's about protecting yourself, your business and your assets so that even if the worst happens, everything will be safe."

After sitting silently for a few seconds, I asked him, "So what would you suggest I do?"

Steve told me to set up *Keen Kleen* as a limited company, so that if anybody tried to take legal action against us, they would have to sue the business, protecting me personally. It would have been very easy for me to turn round to Steve and tell him that I didn't need his help and didn't appreciate him trying to sell me his legal services either. But that would have been a huge mistake. As it happened, several years down the line people did try to start malicious lawsuits against us. Thankfully, they all failed, vindicating the fact that we'd done nothing wrong. If I'd ignored Steve's advice though, a few minor inconveniences could have become major personal financial crises.

There's no point trying a DIY approach when it comes to building a growing business. Many people are hugely successful freelancers and love the lifestyle that self-employment gives them. They fully deserve every bit of success they enjoy. When you're managing teams operating across multiple sites though, you can't operate without external advice. There's too much risk of you getting things wrong and costing yourself a fortune later down the line. Steve was also key in helping me to write business contracts that put *Keen Kleen* in an excellent position, despite being relative newcomers. I'd learnt enough from my experiences with Mr Wheatley to risk another series of bad deals.

Like many moments throughout my business career, the opportunity to agree a deal that would support *Keen Kleen* for years came from a phone call. This time, the voice on the other end of the line was my cousin Phillip's. He got on very well with Tony Beamish, who managed tendering processes for *Virgin Trains*. They were looking for a new contractor to clean *Coventry*, *Birmingham New Street* and *Wolverhampton* railway stations.

Phillip had some of the most amazing news I'd heard for a while.

"Lloyd, I can get you in if you want but the walkaround in Coventry is next week, so I need to know now."

"That would be absolutely awesome, thank you so much!" was my reply without thinking twice.

# Never just follow the crowd...

When I got to *Coventry Station*, I came into my own. All the other cleaning companies' representatives just walked around, looked polite and gave Tony their flashy marketing materials before heading back to the office and expecting him to give them a call. People just thought of tendering as a bit of extra paperwork. They assumed that the biggest businesses would get the best contracts anyway and just saw the walkaround as a polite bit of theatre. Some of the Midlands' biggest names in the FM sector didn't even

## Shifting barriers

send a senior representative to attend the walkaround because nobody cared about building a relationship with Tony. I thought differently and did something revolutionary on the day: actually asking Tony questions. In fact, we had such a good chat that it seemed as though nobody else was there. The conversation couldn't have gone any better and a month or so later, Tony awarded us the contract.

But there was a problem.

It was a problem so big that it even interrupted the celebrations in the office as we heard the news. The contract on offer wasn't very good - and that's being diplomatic. While the £68k per year in revenue it would generate for three years was huge at the time, the rail giant's payment terms threatened to make the contract impossible for us to service profitably. Standard payment terms were 60 days from the invoice date. In order to clean the stations covered by the deal, *Keen Kleen* would need to hire extra operatives, and they all required payment every 30 days. If I accepted *Virgin*'s terms we would be plunged into debt. If, however, I turned down the deal, then *Keen Kleen* would take a colossal reputational hit. Short of both time and options, I asked Steve for advice.

He said, "Can you change the contract, so that *Virgin* gets a discount if they pay you monthly?"

That was some of the best advice I ever heard.

Given the strong rapport that I was building with Tony, I hoped that he might be open to the idea.

I rang him and said, "Thanks so much for choosing to work with us, Tony. We would, of course, be delighted to accept, but need to make a slight tweak to the contract."

An aghast "What???" came back down the line. "You do realise that this is one of the most sought-after tenders in the industry? 50 people wanted this deal. Why should we change it for a startup?"

"I know," was my immediate reply, giving off about 10x more confidence than I felt. "We want to do a sublime job for you for many years to come. We don't see this just as a one-time deal but as a long-term partnership. To give you the world-class service you deserve, we need to bring in some of the most talented people from across the region. They need paying every 30 days. Some of them are single parents, and if they don't get paid on time, they'll really struggle with bills. I would never want someone to work with us and then worry about keeping the lights on."

## No Problem is Permanent

There was a brief pause...

"*I understand that and appreciate your care for your wider team. So, what do you suggest?*" asked Tony, who had recovered his composure after realising that I was coming from a good place.

"We'd like to offer you a 3% discount on all invoices, if you agree to pay us on the 7th of each month. That would mean we could guarantee that everyone working for us across your sites will get paid on time. Then they'll come to work happy and motivated every day. Everybody wins!"

"Thanks for bringing this up, Lloyd, that makes complete sense, but I can't approve it myself. I'll have to talk to our Head Office..." was his candid but reserved reply.

The few days that followed were nerve-racking, to say the least. As we hadn't signed the deal yet, there was a chance that Tony might offer it to someone else. Equally, their Head Office could say no, leaving me having to explain to our team why we'd just lost more than £200k in guaranteed revenue over the next three years. That would be the last thing any of them wanted to hear.

Thankfully, Tony eventually phoned me back with the best possible news: "Head Office were impressed by your ethical approach and would be delighted to agree to your suggestion, providing that you give us a 4% discount on every invoice."

After a bit more haggling and toing and froing, I got that discount down to 3.5% and we signed the deal.

*Virgin* was then spared the 3.5% price increase across our services which came into force for our other clients a few days later.

It would have been an easy mistake to suddenly go on an ego trip and try to do everything myself when Tony first told me that we'd won the original tender. Stepping back and taking Steve's advice meant that I took myself out of the equation and did what was best for the business as a whole, the thriving businesses we supported and our office team. Big deals don't erase your weaknesses. Annoyingly, they tend to have quite an inconvenient habit of projecting those weaknesses into full view. Realising that early on and delegating appropriately will save (and make) you a lot of money. At the same time, try to work on your weaknesses to ensure that you're always giving the best possible impression of your business. Like many business owners, I've put particular effort into working on my public speaking skills.

Shifting barriers

There was a risk that my nervousness in speaking about my business might have made my request to Tony indecisive and ultimately ineffective. I set about fixing that nervousness almost unknowingly early after setting up *Keen Kleen*, thanks to my friends at *BNI*. Every week, each member had to stand up in front of 50 people and talk about their business for at least a minute. Every few weeks, it was also my turn to give a five or ten-minute presentation in front of the whole room. Building personal relationships was one thing: I'd always been good at that. I can chat to anyone and actively enjoy learning about their lives and experiences, but promoting an organisation that seemed to be growing by the day was a completely different kettle of fish. Now, every time I spoke about *Keen Kleen*, it wasn't just myself, *M* and our immediate office team who would benefit from sales boosts. The dozens of people we worked with across different sites counted on me to speak confidently every time I promoted *Keen Kleen*. Imagine that. One slip-up in your talk; one potential referee who gets put off and decides not to give you an intro; one bored phone scroll – and someone else's livelihood could be at risk.

It's difficult to put that level of pressure into words. I wouldn't have changed the position I was in for the world though and still feel hugely grateful for the lifestyle that the business world has given me.

# Great deals come from better relationships...

The first time I stood in front of the room on my first visit to a *BNI* meeting I was almost lost for words. It was difficult enough to make myself heard above the wall of noise in the room, let alone say something captivating.

"Hello, I'm Lloyd Ansermoz and I run *Keen Kleen*. We clean commercial premises across the West Midlands-" seemed like a decent start.

Marketing people would later tell me that I needed to start with a benefit instead of a description, but at the time, I just wanted to get through the speech. There was a slight pause while I thought of what to say next. Despite my best intentions to hide it, everyone could see how nervous I was. The pause continued.

## No Problem is Permanent

Then, a wonderful voice piped up from the back of the room: "What kind of premises do you clean, Lloyd? My mate was asking if I knew any reliable cleaning businesses last week. He needs his factory cleaned."

That was the nicest thing that I could have hoped anyone in the room would do. They could have just booed me off when I paused mid-speech, but that wasn't what this group was about. Everyone was there to help each to grow their businesses. I replied with a big "thank you!" before giving a brief rundown of some of the industrial sites and offices we'd cleaned. Then I sat back down and decided to join the group as a member. Over time, different members would help me with my speaking skills out of the kindness of their hearts. They knew that my team always maintained sites in immaculate condition and encouraged me to share that confidently with the world. Eventually, my skills improved and those weekly speeches became a breeze. Compliments on my 5 and 10-minute talks from friendly faces within the group followed regularly.

I highly doubt I would have been able to get through such a high-pressure series of conversations with Tony successfully with so much at stake for *Keen Kleen* without this group's support. Tony and I would end up becoming very good friends. He never regretted giving me a slightly amended deal. In fact, *Virgin* expanded their partnership with us, appointing us to clean every one of their stations from London Euston to Carlisle for the next three years. We even negotiated all-access first-class rail passes for me and a few of my colleagues too. That was one of the best ideas that Pete ever had. It all started when he needed to attend a meeting with *Virgin* in Coventry.

"Who's going to pay my expenses?" he asked.

"What expenses?" I asked rather too dismissively. "It hardly costs anything to get to Coventry."

"If you're going for a one-off trip!" he clarified quite sternly. "I need to visit teams there every week or so and then visit other sites after that too. When you add all the tickets together, this job gets quite expensive."

"Sorry, Pete, you're right-" was the only answer I could give to that. "Rather than the ticket costs coming out of *Keen Kleen*'s budget, I'll ask Tony if we can have a few free passes covering all of their stations. It's in everybody's interests that you can attend meetings as easily as possible."

Shifting barriers

That made sense to the *Virgin* team, who then gave our team the free passes covering all of their services to share. That was a massive help and saved us a fortune in travel costs across the country.
The prospect of my Midlands-based business servicing sites across the whole of England felt like an impossible dream only a few months beforehand. Thanks to some of the hardest-working and most talented site managers and cleaning operatives I've ever had the privilege of working with, everything ran smoothly and our hard work was getting noticed by *Virgin*'s executives. I'll never forget Tony's kind invitation to attend lunch with Sir Richard Branson and other executives to celebrate the launch of the then cutting-edge, top of the market *Pendolino* service. Sir Richard walked in as if he was catching up with his mates over a casual meal. I was expecting him to have an absolutely massive entourage – but he wouldn't have any of that. It was an honour to sit next to one of the most successful and modest entrepreneurs that the UK has ever produced. As I tucked into my filet mignon, memories of the sandwiches I used to eat out of my lunchbox when cleaning cellars all those years ago were almost as vivid as the lovely restaurant that present company were all enjoying. Then, it hit me. Times really were different now. *Keen Kleen* was changing not just my life, but was providing meaningful, long-term jobs for dozens of people too.
Pressure felt like a thing of the past. I knew that if I could win new business then our amazing team and the strength of our corporate partnerships could handle anything that the world threw at us. Even more leads started coming in from our reputation, growing profile and my ever-improving public speaking skills. Noel suggested I put those skills to the test as soon as our agreement with *Virgin* allowed us to make news of the national deal public.
"You've got to announce this at *BNI*!" he insisted. "Everyone will be so proud."
I wasn't sure how they would react. "Won't they just think I'm showing off?" I asked him, nervously.
"No, not at all!" replied Noel in one of the most reassuring voices I'd ever heard. "They'll love it!"
So, at our next meeting, I announced the deal and everyone's response completely blew me away. The room erupted as everyone stood up and started cheering almost as loudly as Pete had at those awards ceremonies. I insisted that this success was a

## No Problem is Permanent

team effort, but they wouldn't stop celebrating me. It was a huge privilege to see a whole room full of people so genuinely happy for me. That moment will stay with me forever. The nerves of my first meeting had been replaced by complete trust. I knew that everyone in that room was looking out for me and trying to find exciting new business opportunities for the *Keen Kleen* team. My *BNI* friends' reactions that day made me trust my colleagues even more too. Their tireless work had produced a response from a room of business owners that never would have been possible if I was doing everything on my own.

Trusting my teams gave me more time to focus on what I'd always been great at. Identifying the key decision makers in clients' businesses and building strong relationships with them. Kate and Jenny were two of *Virgin*'s most wonderful people. As buyers, their jobs involved signing off dozens of invoices for payment each month. I needed them to approve all of our invoices as an absolute priority. Any delay could wreck our cash flow and leave me having to explain to some very upset operatives why they wouldn't get paid on time. Although my agreement with Tony of payment on the 7th of the month was still going strong, the slightest admin delay could push that date back.

If invoices aren't approved, they don't get paid.

The larger the company you're dealing with, the more stages you have to go through to get that approval. That's just the way it works. I didn't make the rules, I just had to live with them as a still fairly new business owner.

Every month, I made sure I took both Kate and Jenny out for a delicious lunch in one of Birmingham's most boutique restaurants. We picked a different restaurant each month just to vary things a bit. *Keen Kleen* paid for everything and our lunches often lasted the whole afternoon. Nothing was ever too much and we enjoyed some wonderful meals. One of the things that made these lunches so enjoyable was that we never discussed business. We talked about our families, kids and interests outside of work (*Villa* came up more than a few times). The whole point of them was to thank Kate and Jenny for their continuing support, not to try to sell their employer more services.

That happened naturally beforehand. I would often meet them at their offices inside New Street station and then we'd head over to a restaurant. One time on the way out of the office, they started telling me about some terrible trouble they'd been having with people slipping on one of the station's bridges. I asked them what

## Shifting barriers

barrier matting they used. The answer was that they hadn't thought that such a simple solution could solve what felt like a real headache of a problem. I happened to know a quality barrier mat producer and suggested that this might be a problem that could be solved in a phone call. A few weeks later, *Keen Kleen* was managing the barrier matting across all of the stations we cleaned for them. The mat producer gave me a price, I added 30% to it and sent *Virgin* the bill. Kate and Jenny were all too happy to take this urgent problem off their to-do lists, and I was delighted to be making 30% pure profit on a new and popular service that absorbed very little of my time. Our matting partner did all the heavy lifting and my work essentially stopped when the deal was finalised. Again, a team effort grew my business far more than I ever could have dreamt of achieving alone. Business owners achieve far more through delegating than dictating.

Despite all of the business we were doing with one particular rail giant, *Keen Kleen* still wasn't maintaining all of the biggest railway stations in the Midlands and beyond. What's now the Chiltern Mainline (known locally as the 'scenic route') connects Birmingham's *Snow Hill Station* with *London Marylebone*. Solihull and Leamington Spa are among the many lovely stops on this route. In the early years of *Keen Kleen*, the majority of that line was operated by *Central Trains* and maintained by one of our biggest competitors. I had always wanted to add *Snow Hill* and the stations it services to our collection of sites, but didn't have a contact at *Central Trains*. Fortunately, I didn't need one as the phone rang again with perfect timing. Jack Hayward, who looked after their tendering processes, called our office and wanted to speak urgently. *Central Trains* needed to modernise their busiest stations quickly, and part of that modernisation required significantly upgrading their washroom facilities. On visiting Jack at *Snow Hill*, it was obvious to me that they also needed barrier matting just as urgently. The main ramp which still forms the entrance to *Snow Hill* was becoming a major slipping hazard.

Almost as soon as I'd arrived, Jack got straight into the nitty-gritty of what he was having to deal with every day.

"Lloyd, I don't know where to begin. We need our stations cleaned, we need barrier matting like New Street, we need Sani Bins, Air Fresheners, Changing Tables, new soap dispensers. Where am I going to get all of this stuff quickly at a sensible price?"

## No Problem is Permanent

Looking down at my slightly dampened shoes - while trying not to slip on the floor mid-meeting - gave me ample thinking time.

"There's any easy fix for that. How about we provide you with all of those services across all of your stations as part of an all-in-one deal?"

I saw the panic vanish from Jack's eyes almost instantly as he gave me a reply that I normally loved hearing:

"Yes, that's exactly what we need. When can you start?"

This time was slightly different though, as the deal I'd mentioned didn't exist yet. Because I got on so well with the team at *Virgin*, they paid for the barrier matting in accordance with our existing terms. That wasn't a given with every train company though. With more and more products and services being added to our offering, including brand-new *Washroom Services*, there was an increasing risk of invoices being separated and payments we were due being delayed. On top of that, more services meant more operatives who needed paying quickly. Striking a deal to source a range of washroom products was easy: I just copied the barrier mats deal with the relevant companies. It looked like the tricky bit would be paying all of them and all of our operatives on time.

Steve came to the rescue yet again.

He suggested, "Just amend your contracts to wrap everything together in the same invoice and get it paid by the 7th of each month."

I'd been so wrapped up in trying to entertain our existing clients and build new relationships that this brilliant solution had completely passed me by. *Central* were more than happy to agree to these terms and Steve's magic worked so well that our office was quickly overwhelmed by other companies wanting similar deals.

Our busy admin team was looking for new ways to streamline things, and one of the best receptionists I ever worked with had a lightbulb moment:

"Why don't we just create a shopping list where clients can pick the extras they want, tick them off the form and send it back to us?"

So we did, and our *Washroom Services* grew and grew from there. Not every innovation has to come from the MD's office. Never make the mistake of ignoring a colleague's idea just because they're not currently working in a senior role. If you had no receptionists for the day back then, your business was knackered. The internet wasn't a big thing then. Everything came in through the phone and calls couldn't ever go unanswered.

Staying open to new ideas keeps you open to new revenue streams and quick wins that might have gone over your head otherwise. Don't let a personal mental barrier around company hierarchy block potential huge profitability for your business. Never look to cut costs on legal advice either; you'll need it more and more as your business grows.

# Sometimes you outgrow your partners...

As invaluable as Steve's advice was in getting *Keen Kleen* off the ground, our rapid growth meant that we needed additional legal expertise. Fergal Dowling was a well-known expert in HR law and had just joined a top national firm's Birmingham office. His support was vital to the next stage of our growth. As well as seeing off those malicious claims that Steve had seen coming from some of the staff we inherited, Fergal suggested giving every member of our team a staff handbook. This handbook covered what they could expect from us but also what we expected of them, and where the law stood. I would never have thought to even ask our design team to make a staff handbook, let alone stack it with so many valuable legal insights. Fergal's firm did the whole thing, I just picked up the handbooks and made sure that everybody got one.

I've avoided using the word suppliers to describe people like Steve, and later, Fergal, because that wouldn't do them justice by half. Yes, they provided us with quality services - that was a given. They did so much more and meant so much more to us than that though. They and many others formed a crucial support system as we grew. They were all our partners.

But sadly, nothing changes the fact that sometimes you outgrow your partners. We reached a point where *Keen Kleen* needed Fergal and his firm to handle all of our legal affairs, not just advise us on HR law. Likewise, when I came to sell *Fidelis* many years later, we needed a specialist M&A firm to handle that transaction. That's not to say that you don't hugely appreciate the help that partners gave you at particular moments during your

## No Problem is Permanent

business journey. It just means that you've reached a stage of that journey where you need different advice so that you can analyse different situations accurately.

The same happened with my search for a business coaching programme that evolved as my business did. I will never be able to thank Chris Barrow enough for the support he gave me as I adjusted from star salesman to business owner. But unfortunately, I found that his advice stayed the same as my business grew. As dozens of talented colleagues turned into a few hundred there were new pressures on my time and new challenges, as well as new and increasingly complex projects to manage. Laurence Udell would become my new Obi-One Kenobi as we moved into a completely different sector. I had never imagined myself becoming a property investor in my wildest dreams. But the opportunity arose and thankfully, *Keen Kleen* had enough cash in the bank to take full advantage of it.

Just as I had hoped when first meeting Howard (and he had too) that 'kitchen refurb' loan had launched a hugely successful business into the world. The track-record that other bankers had sneeringly dismissed a few years beforehand had been well and truly proven. Thanks to the support of our wonderful partners, *Keen Kleen* had moved from survival to expansion. We were about to find ourselves in a whole new industry even if that industry's business leaders weren't quite ready to accept us...

# Chapter Seven

## Still an outsider

"Excuse us, Mr Ansermoz…We'll try to be as quiet as possible," said the eighth camera operator to clatter through my office that hour.

I was trying to be as kind and understanding as possible, but the media team really was making an absolute racket. They stayed for the whole day too. The team had come from the BBC and were interviewing me as part of a piece on business growth in the Midlands. They wanted some ideas about what the government could do to help businesses like ours. My answers to the questions in what turned out (after all that) to only be a three-minute interview segment were less straightforward than they would have been a year earlier. *Keen Kleen* had done so well that I'd ended up in a sector I hadn't even dreamt of dipping my toe into when I was younger: property. We weren't just dabbling either. When the TV

No Problem is Permanent

crew arrived, I was the proud owner of a serviced-office building, having started *Keen Kleen* in my kitchen only a few years earlier. Months before that special moment, our team was growing and needed an entire floor of office space. There wasn't a huge amount of space like that on the market and the lovely office we'd enjoyed for the previous year or so was getting a bit cramped. Fortunately, my friend needed some help, the new space we needed became available, and an opportunity for a new and very profitable business came into view.

## Ownership on ice...

My friend John had made a fortune leasing Tropical Ice machines to a whole range of venues. Arcades, cinemas, supermarkets, leisure centres, swimming pools, social clubs: you name it, they had one. Tropical Ice was a very British take on American slushies and gave you a delicious, refreshing drink that was the tastiest possible cross between frozen yoghurt and ice cream. Everybody wanted one and therefore, John was earning thousands in rent every day. He used this money to build an impressive property portfolio. The crown jewel of this collection was a serviced-office block which had promised impressive long-term returns. The problem for John was that returns only reach your account and stay there if tenants pay rent on time and maintain their offices in excellent condition. That hadn't been happening and John was now emotionally exhausted.

He phoned me and explained the situation. "Lloyd, I don't know what to do. Some of our tenants haven't paid us in six months and their offices are in a disgraceful condition. I can't get rid of them and the hole in our books is just growing and growing. I'm hugely busy with the Tropical Ice business and this problem is just robbing way too much of my time. I'm losing more and more time and money by the day."

I wanted the building as I knew that our *Keen Kleen* team could make a profit out of it. Many of our contacts were looking for new office spaces and, more importantly, they were trusted friends who we could rely on to be responsible tenants. The quicker they replaced the current nightmare tenants, the better.

I also wanted to help John, who had always been happy to offer advice and introductions as I was getting *Keen Kleen* off the ground. He was a good man and didn't deserve the disrespect that

## Still an outsider

many of his tenants were showing him. The whole situation was out of order really. I offered to have a look and see what I could do for him. When I went through the books, the situation was even worse than I'd first thought. The costs of owning the building were gnawing away at John's Tropical Ice fortune and if things didn't improve rapidly within the next few months, he was facing a disaster. A sale seemed inevitable, but nobody would want to buy a building with that many problem tenants for anything like its true value, leaving him facing huge losses.

After going through everything, I phoned John back and asked him straight-up, "How much do you want for the whole building?"

He replied by saying "That's a very kind offer, Lloyd but I really need your help in recovering these bad debts and finding good tenants. When things are back on a level-footing, I may be able to sell the building to some investors."

Here was another business owner who wanted my skills but didn't value those skills enough to see me as their professional equal. To describe knowing that as 'not a great feeling' would be a huge understatement. However, I knew that unless the debts were recovered sharpish, there wouldn't be a building to own.

So, I suggested what seemed like a great compromise: "How about if *Keen Kleen* moves into the building, helps to collect the rent, and you give us a cut of everything that comes in?"

John's voice lifted about a foot. "If you can do that," he exclaimed, "*Keen Kleen* can have an office for free. I'll go one better than giving you that floor you're after - you can have the top one. It's been available for weeks and I've not had any serious interest from anyone decent."

That would have to do for the time being.

We moved in, the problem tenants moved out and John started receiving the returns he'd been due for so long (with some left over for us too). We also pursued historic debts and eventually managed to recover a chunk of almost half a year's unpaid rent from various tenants after they'd left. Fergal was there to ensure that we did everything by the book (whilst actually getting things done).

My hope was that after seeing all of this progress, John would change his mind and be more than happy to sell us the building. Unfortunately, that was a hope too far and our success in turning the building didn't seem to matter one bit. While John appreciated both this turnaround and the success that *Keen Kleen* had achieved in a relatively short space of time, he still didn't see me as his 'sort' of businessman. Sadly, some of the negative attitudes about cleaning as an industry (that I would experience again on that unforgettable phone call to *Fidelis* from the engineering company) seemed to follow me around wherever I went. It didn't matter that by the time I moved into John's building, *Keen Kleen* employed well over 100 people. In his eyes, and the eyes of many others, I would always be a 'cleaner' and should stick to maintaining buildings - not owning them. It felt as though no matter how much I succeeded as an entrepreneur, no matter how many people I employed, lives I changed and how much tax I paid, some people just didn't think that 'someone like me' should be in the same meetings and rooms as them.

It wasn't something that came over in a directly offensive way - none of the other business owners I met while building *Keen Kleen* ever told me directly that I "Shouldn't" have certain goals and ambitions. They just assumed that I "Wouldn't". It was as if I was just expected to be happy making money and that ought to be enough for me. It wasn't.

# Building more than bank balances...

17 year-old Lloyd was delighted just to be picking up a wage. The version of Lloyd who moved in John's building wanted much more than that. My focus had become creating generational wealth for myself and my wider team, not just in a materialistic sense, but spiritual wealth too. Yes, everyone wanted nice houses and cars and nobody wanted the entire *Keen Kleen* team to get to that point in their lives more than me. But that wasn't all. The more I was learning about business-building, the more I wanted to encourage my team to think carefully about the values driving them. Even if someone only worked with us for a short time, it was hugely important for me that they entered a happy working environment which respected them and helped them to build invaluable skills for the rest of their careers. I constantly learnt from them too. Every member of our team added something different and brought experiences that only improved my commercial and cultural awareness. We all needed to grow together as a team while keeping *Keen Kleen*'s financial performance moving in the same positive direction.

## Still an outsider

Part of that process involved broadening my business portfolio into other sectors. This expansion would give colleagues the chance to grow their skills in new areas, while increasing our revenue and adding some extra strings to my bow too. I felt like buying the building from John would give me a prized seat at that executive table, as well as providing *Keen Kleen* with a whole host of new benefits.

Despite his obvious need to sell, weeks turned into months and he still wouldn't sell to me. I did eventually end up buying the building though. The pure anxiety caused by all of those nightmare tenants had taken its toll on John and, very sadly, his wider health began to suffer.

Even with my team managing the building, and new tenants in situ, its ownership still absorbed far more of John's time than he was happy to give. Property investment was supposed to be a smart way to grow wealth gained from his real passion - seeing how happy those Tropical Ice machines made families around the country. Instead, the building had become a difficult distraction which sapped energy away from what he really loved.

Despite the tensions between us, we both wanted each other to be happy. Selling the building became the only way to achieve that shared goal. Nobody else knew the building as well as I did and, more importantly, nobody else was willing to pay John what I was offering. A quick call to my old friend and mentor and now investor, Noel, ensured that we had the funds in place to complete the purchase. Then things moved forwards from there. I was immensely proud to become Noel's business partner. An inspirational business leader who I'd looked up to was now my colleague. After the purchase had gone through, John held onto an office in the building for a bit longer. Eventually though, he fully moved on and left the building.

I still remember what he said to me as he cleared out his office for the last time:

"Lloyd, I hope this building gives you a happiness that it never gave me."

Thankfully, his other business continued to deliver him far more than the building ever had.

I marked the shift into a brand-new sector by launching a brand-new business. *Keen Kleen* couldn't manage a diverse range of cleaning requirements and property rentals under the same brand. Plus, there was a significant tax advantage in paying rent to another business (which I happened to own). This extra bill would add a cost to *Keen Kleen*'s annual accounts without costing me a penny.

*KMS* was born to offer appropriate office space to *Keen Kleen* and a whole range of other businesses. A major social care provider took the first floor. Word went round that if your business was thriving, you needed an office in our building and a large waiting list quickly followed. As the internet became big and a new generation of businesses started launching, the *KMS* website went up and I put the rockstar receptionist who had come up with the 'shopping list' idea in charge of managing the building. The builders' yard units next to our building became the next big *KMS* purchase, mainly as somewhere to store *Keen Kleen*'s fleet of vans for free, but also to build up a nice revenue stream from parking fees.

It seemed as though I was finally where I wanted to be in life. The lad who jumped at the chance of extra shifts at the bakery and became a star salesman had now become an established business owner with a diversifying range of interests and a massive and ever-growing team. After years of seeking validation, it felt like I finally had it in the palm of my hand. The initial call from the BBC and then the interview seemed like the latest huge achievement on a journey that was just getting better and better. I wish I could have bottled the happiness I felt in that moment, as it would have sold for a fortune. Sadly though, sometimes you can get so caught up in some things that you miss others and I missed a glaringly obvious fact: everything I'd built was slowly crashing around me.

# Growing apart...

*M* struggled to appreciate my determination to go beyond enjoying a comfortable lifestyle and constantly make new business contacts. My friendships with Noel, Chris, Mark and Howard had given me a level of financial understanding that neither of us had enjoyed growing up. There just wasn't access to that kind of knowledge back then unless you'd either lived through relevant experiences or came from certain backgrounds. Neither of us ticked either of those boxes. *M* felt that the people I was investing so much time in weren't 'like us'. It felt like just as I was finally becoming much more of an insider in the business world, I was becoming an outsider in my own marriage. She thought I was

## Still an outsider

constantly wasting time reading business books and attending networking events.

She used to say, "Sell to the people you meet at these things, but don't hang out with them, who cares what they know so long as they pay our invoices on time."

I'd lived that life when I was with Tracey. My focus back then was on flash cars and jackets rather than lifelong learning and financial growth. The result had been that I ended up back at square one, with no assets and living with my parents again. There was absolutely no way I was going back to that life of spending money now and thinking about the future later.

One of the biggest challenges of launching a business with your other half is that you both need to share the same ambitions throughout your journey. It's not just your personal business journey anymore; the two have merged into one and that makes managing the inevitable bumps in the road that come with growing a business even tougher. At one time, our goals were the same. *M* and I wanted to work as hard as we possibly could in order to improve our lives. While we were franchisees building what became *Keen Kleen* on the side of working for Mr Wheatley, we'd really just given ourselves hugely demanding jobs rather than starting our own business. Back then, that was fine because we were beginning to build futures that wouldn't have been possible if we hadn't taken that leap into franchising. The same thing applied when I was working with *Indepth*. I had an even bigger job, a nice new salary and was constantly learning about business and entrepreneurship. At the same time, she continued building on our franchising work, picked up more and more cleaning clients and needed Mr Wheatley's brand recognition less and less.

Then everything changed.

*Keen Kleen*'s growth from 2000-2007 was bigger than either of us could ever have imagined. Not everybody is ready for that kind of change in their lives. It's one thing to talk about financial literacy and work on money management, but putting those ideas into practice becomes significantly tougher when more money than you ever dreamt of earning lands in your account every week.

The person I went into business with never stopped working. There wasn't a shift she wouldn't work, a place she wouldn't go or a job she wouldn't take to improve our financial situation. But when *Keen Kleen* was booming, *M* was barely in the office. When she did come in, it usually wasn't followed by a significant boost

85

## No Problem is Permanent

in team morale. I remember sitting at my desk and trying to hold the phone particularly carefully, so that the client on the other end of the line wouldn't hear the cacophony of shouting coming from the room next door. We hadn't quite built our client relationships into ideal partnerships yet; that would come with *Fidelis*. Optimism for the future wasn't at the top of my mind in my *Keen Kleen* office at that moment. All my focus was on trying to block out the scene next door.

"How long do you need to spend on that toilet?" was *M*'s furious complaint to one of our team members who was battling coeliac disease. This wonderful person immediately burst into floods of tears.

"I...d...didn't know we got timed on toilet breaks..." she sobbed.

"Do you think we're paying you to be in the toilet!" screamed *M*. "If I wanted to chuck £10 down the loo, I'd go in there and do it myself!"

*M* never used to be like that.

When we brought in our first few team members, my then wife couldn't have been warmer, happier or more supportive of their long-term personal and professional growth. Now though, all that happy atmosphere had turned ice cold. This particular row wasn't about loo breaks. It was the latest in a series of protests against my growth plans for the business.

Many far less printable things started becoming regular features in an office atmosphere which was becoming increasingly tense and uncomfortable whenever she walked in. I felt completely stuck. *M* didn't want me to become the person I wanted to be, and my business peers wouldn't truly accept me as one of them if I became the person who she wanted me to be. In fact, I couldn't have accepted myself becoming that person either. The feeling of being so close to but so far from my goals had never seemed realer or more searing.

As the person who I'd gone into business with lost motivation and gave up any real role in pushing growth forwards, I asked myself what I could have done differently to help her avoid the situation when formally setting up *Keen Kleen*. Like anyone in a bad situation, asking this question is only natural. I think the answer would have been to start preparing for the rapid growth the business would experience years before I did. Again, hindsight is a wonderful thing. There's no way I could have predicted back in 2000 how much *Keen Kleen*'s rise would change both *M* and

## Still an outsider

myself and how far that change would force us apart. I was so busy pursuing the validation of success that came with thriving teams, big contracts, awards dinners and TV interviews back then that I forgot one crucial thing: defining what that success would really look like and the impact it would have on our lives. Like many entrepreneurs, I only truly realised the difference between giving yourself a job and building an asset that you can sell after starting my business.

I felt like I was genuinely learning something new and growing into the role every day but made a whole series of huge mistakes along the way. One of the worst was disrespecting one of my most trusted colleagues, Steve, in front of the entire team.

The CEO of one of the UK's fastest-growing businesses phoned with infuriating news.

"Lloyd, I'm appalled. One of your colleagues has just used a grievously offensive word against me. Some feedback about the quality of their work was met by a tirade of abuse and then this most indecent language. I don't expect to see Steve at any of our sites again. Furthermore, I expect a significant reduction in your fees to compensate me for this distressing incident."

All I could do was apologise and assure them that the matter would be dealt with internally. Then, I stormed out of my office and confronted Steve immediately. He was just heading off.

"STEVE, where do you think you're going? What makes you think you have the right to talk to our valued partners like that? You're an absolute disgrace. You've embarrassed me, embarrassed us and potentially cost us a fortune in fees. What do you think you're playing at?" I fumed.

Steve just stood there silently and looked at me like he'd bumped into a total stranger on the way out of work. "Lloyd, he's lying. I never said that. You should know I would never say that. Why would you believe him over me?"

"OK, let's go and clear this up together then!" I replied, defensively. "We'll go and ask him together and see what he says. If he's telling the truth though, the discount we'll have to give them is coming out of your wages!"

I should never have threatened that. It was so wrong. I should have just trusted Steve. When we spoke to the CEO in question at the meeting, Steve was proved right. While they had exchanged some fairly frank views in a tense conversation, all the provocation had come from the CEO, who was being hugely

unreasonable. Most importantly, the CEO admitted that he had lied. Steve never used the offensive word in question.
"It wasn't that big of a deal, in fairness," said a now much more relaxed CEO. "I just wanted a discount."
I had a massive apology to make. I apologised to Steve both personally and in front of the whole office after kicking off at him completely wrongly. Thankfully, he forgave me.
Redemption and forgiveness are fundamental aspects of business life. If you can't admit when you're in the wrong and make things right, then you won't get very far. You'll lose great colleagues and cost yourself a fortune in the long-term.
Sadly, my half of the business partnership that founded *Keen Kleen* understood that far more than the other. Long-running grudges and drama don't help anyone in business or in life.

# A new path…

I eventually confided in Laurence for advice and he told me something truly profound:
"Lloyd, everybody changes. That's part of life. Most entrepreneurs will be interrupted from detailed Board discussions about helping 200+ people to grow by their alarm clocks. You get interrupted from those meetings by calls from some of the UK's biggest companies who happen to also be your long-term clients. Some of the people you're associating yourself with are holding you back from being the managing director that you could be. People are either in or they're out. There's too much negativity lingering around your business and I'm worried that it's stopping you from truly achieving everything that you're capable of. It might be a good idea to make some changes to your team."
I wasn't quite sure how to reply to that. My office team (who I spent the most time with every day) generally seemed quite positive and life after *Keen Kleen* seemed much further off. Lots of families still depended on the business for their incomes, so I was willing to give the few colleagues who weren't positively contributing to *Keen Kleen*'s growth opportunities to change.
Eventually I asked Laurence, "Who do you think should move on from *Keen Kleen*? More importantly, who would replace them? It's already difficult enough to get other executives to fully accept me and I don't want to make things worse by making it look like

## Still an outsider

my business is mired in uncertainty. It took me long enough to get this far."

"Lloyd," said Laurence, "It's not for me to tell you who to hire or who to let go. Focus on the key principles that you need anybody in your inner-circle to stick to: loyalty, kindness, honesty and hard work. If people aren't displaying these qualities, then perhaps it's time for them to move on. In terms of replacements, you know so many talented professionals in the industry that I'm sure wonderful individuals with gravitate towards you. Do what's right for your team and you'll do the right thing for the business too. Focus less on opinions and more on motives. If someone is going to be a part of your team, you need everything they're saying to come from a positive and constructive place. The people you bring in or continue working alongside don't have to conform to external assumptions of what makes a good team. They just have to present the best mix of skills and mindset to help your team progress."

Sometimes being an outsider has its advantages. At the end of each day, if you can do right by your team, and they do right by each other, then you've had a very good day at the office (even if that office is virtual). Thanks to support from Laurence and others, I learnt to stop worrying about outside opinions and focused on creating a Happiness-Centred Business instead. Those awesome friends showed me that my purpose was to take the lead in creating and spreading happiness wherever I could. That meant retaining faith in even the most difficult of circumstances. When somebody hurts you, it's only natural to lose faith in people's good intentions. A huge challenge for me was to react differently and not let my struggles with *M* and a few other colleagues cloud my faith in the goodness in people. Drawing inspirational teachings from business leaders whose ideas I read and studied, such as Tony Robbins, Deepak Chopra, Paddi Lund, Kiyosaki and Lechter played an enormous role in helping me to put Laurence's advice into practice.

"No problem is permanent" is one of Tony's quotes that has helped steer me through so much. There's always a tomorrow, always a solution, and always at least one way in which you can improve any situation. He would also play a central role in a life-changing trip to California months later.

I wish I'd known many years before arriving in California that pursuing my purpose meant so much than just receiving validation from others. When everything's going well, you tend not to reflect

## No Problem is Permanent

on life that deeply though. It's only when life descends into a bewildering and almost endless journey downhill that you grab whatever time you can to stop and reflect on the fundamentals that really matter to you. As *Keen Kleen*'s growth began to stall, my immediate goal was to try to bring some stability to the business and get things back on the right path, while *M* and I set off on our own separate ones.

My path did ultimately lead to building the Happiness-Centred Business that I'd always dreamt of leading. Sadly though, that business wasn't *Keen Kleen* and my path to the spiritual success I wanted for so long was far longer and more traumatic than I could have predicted (even in my most pessimistic forecasts). There were times when giving up completely on entrepreneurship felt like my best option. But some things are so important that you can't ever give up on them. When you have the opportunity to help hundreds of people pursue their best lives and achieve goals that they never thought would be possible, that's worth pursuing whatever the cost. Leadership is not a fun, Instagrammable title. It's a lifelong responsibility to enable and empower others to become their best selves. If that makes you come across like a bit of an odd-ball or an outsider, then so be it.

And yes, I do regret not using that line in the BBC interview...

# Chapter Eight

## The end of the beginning

When I was younger everyone around me loved boxing, but nobody could afford a pair of gloves. One day, I took my left-hand glove to school and another lad from my year, Adrian, had a right-hand glove.

We got into a bit of a disagreement and then all we could hear from the other kids in the playground was, "fight, fight, fight!"

All I saw next was a massive right hand heading straight towards my nose:

"Bang!"

It hurt (a lot), I ran home crying and Adrian reeled away in celebration. Everyone else was laughing at me and that just made everything worse.

When I got home my Granda asked me, "What's happened?"

"I've lost a fight in school and I've never been so embarrassed…" I sobbed.

When I'd finally pulled myself together, my Granda told me something that's still relevant today:

"When life knocks you down, you've got to get back up and hit it back. See this sixpence? I'll give it to you if you go back to school right now and give that idiot the punch he deserves."

Fighting shouldn't be part of school life. The lesson here was about far more than that though: any adversity can be overcome if you fight hard enough. I stormed back to school, found Adrian, and challenged him to a rematch. This time, he was the one who ran off. He didn't cause me any trouble after that. In fact, nobody did. Granda couldn't have been prouder when I got back home.

Nowadays, my favourite pair of cufflinks has two sixpences on them. They've travelled with me to Boardrooms, courtrooms and hospitals. Whatever you do, stand your ground, fight your corner and don't give up: those are some of the most important life lessons my Granda taught me.

# The end of the line…

Fighting was the order of the day as *Keen Kleen*'s non-stop success suddenly began to dip. Unfortunately, my relationship with *M* was heading to its end and I had to do everything possible to stop the business going down with it. That was an increasingly difficult task. Contract reviews and renewals had become so expected that we'd changed from being the disruptors to becoming established providers, but all that was now looking very fragile.

My phone rang again and it wasn't good news at all.

Tony Beamish told me, "Lloyd, you've done a great job for us over these last few years, but recently, a few disappointing things have cropped up. Nothing massive, but just service falling short of the high standards we've come to expect from *Keen Kleen*. I've got another company offering me slightly slicker services for a lot less money than you're charging. My bosses want me to go with them, so you're losing the contract. I wanted you to find out from me first. I'm sorry, Lloyd. This isn't a negotiation. The decision's already been made."

"Thanks so much for letting me know, Tony, it's been a pleasure doing business with you-" was all I could think to say.

Then the call ended.

A blessing in disguise

A few minutes later, I was still sitting there in disbelief. A six-figure multi-year deal had just evaporated into thin air in seconds. There was no point trying to argue that one with Tony. He was right. The disruptors had been disrupted. Newer subsidiaries of larger businesses had undercut us and made us look like yesterday's expensive news.

Tony would later leave *Virgin* and thanks to our strong relationship, he came and worked for me at *Keen Kleen* before following me back to *Indepth* and then to *Fidelis* as an operations manager.

Sadly though, the challenges of that time were preventing me from seeing opportunities that would fill my inboxes over the coming years. While no problem is permanent, the issues afflicting *Keen Kleen* were mounting at such a pace that it felt like I was plunged into a permanent series of problems.

After a few days of thinking about how to replace the massive hole that Tony's call had just blown in our turnover, I got some more bad news. Jack Hayward of *Central* had asked just to meet in his office instead of going for our usual monthly lunch. Something seemed off from the minute I walked into his office. He seemed almost sad, as if he was about to read a prepared statement very awkwardly. As it happened, he was:

"Lloyd," Jack began, almost sighing, "I wasn't sure how to put this so I wrote it down. We've had a wonderful time working with you and I've really appreciated your generosity and professionalism. However, some of your operatives just don't seem on it anymore. Other businesses are offering us a slightly better service for far, far less, and my bosses want me to award them the contract. I'm sorry, Lloyd, but *Central* won't be renewing our contract with *Keen Kleen* when it comes to an end next month."

That news hit me like a tonne of bricks.

The emotional toll on the whole team of all the drama in the office was showing in our work right across our portfolio. A seemingly unstoppable rise was coming crashing to a halt. "Is there anything we can do?" I asked somewhat hopefully but knowing what the answer would be.

"No," said Jack, "Sadly, this is it my friend." I shook his hand, walked out and wondered what was happening to the business I'd worked so hard to build.

In the middle of New Street, I got my brand-new mobile phone out and rang *M*, absolutely fuming. "You've just lost us another

## No Problem is Permanent

contract. Why are you ruining everything I built?!! I never want to see you in the office again!" Then, I hung up.

That probably wasn't the best way to deal with it but, as I stood outside in torrential rain, it seemed as though everything going wrong with the business was purely down to *M*. It wasn't, of course.

Our company culture still wasn't quite where I wanted it to be and now firms preferred to work with big multinationals and their subsidiaries instead of a local firm. To compete with that at a higher price point you need absolutely perfect customer service - consistently. We still weren't quite there yet. Sadly, a few of our team had grown complacent. Deadlines for tender submissions came and went. We missed them because some colleagues felt as though the tendering company would end up phoning us anyway. They didn't. One conversation with a colleague about this particularly sticks out in my mind. It happened after I got chatting to a recent hire in our marketing team in the corridor one evening after he had spent all afternoon networking.

"So?" I asked, "Did you pick up any good leads this afternoon?"

"No," he replied, "But we tried some of the most outstanding wines I've ever sampled. The best was a smooth Bordeaux from 20 years ago. The Right Bank wines are hugely underrated, but they taste so good. Do you prefer Left or Right Bank, Lloyd? As wonderful as some of the Right Bank châteaux are, I feel that some of the Left Bank's greatest vintages will never be topped."

"I would have preferred it if you'd developed some business rather than just running up our expenses-" was the closest I could come to a reply (through gritted teeth) without shouting so loudly that the care business downstairs would have become concerned. Shouting at colleagues doesn't do anyone any good.

After a brief pause for breath, I eventually found the words I was looking for.

"You know that things are getting tighter around here and we need some nice, reliable new partners to replace the train companies. How much progress did you make with the tenders this morning?"

His response to this question was somehow even worse.

"The deadline isn't for *weeks*, but I think someone is picking it up. We'll get something in on time and I'll check it over to make sure it's OK before it goes out."

A blessing in disguise

At this point, keeping my cool was becoming slightly harder than doing one of those ice bucket challenges that went viral a few years ago. Nonetheless, I pushed on.

"Do you think that so many of us here have worked 18-hour days for years to create some '*OK*' stuff? Do you think that some of the biggest companies in the country will settle for OK service and *decent* results?" I asked resolutely. "*Keen Kleen* exists to be the best. This isn't just a slogan. We need to be the best. We live to be the best. You might want to think about whether those are the values you're representing next time you're out representing us…and I need those tenders completed to our usual standards soon."

He didn't stay with us for much longer.

Becoming the best is hard enough in good times. In any area of life, you need to keep the same hunger that you had in the beginning - when you were looking to make a name for yourself - when you finally achieve success. Otherwise, pole position will slip through your fingertips. Business is no different. Sadly, with everything else that was going on, it became impossible for me to find the time to coach the complacent members of our team into improving and *Keen Kleen* began staring ever more distantly at the pole position we'd once held. At the time, my horrific situation with *M* absorbed almost all of my thinking space.

# A lonely onward journey…

It felt as though I was fighting with *M*, but I was actually fighting with myself. It's quite difficult for men to share their weaknesses in professional environments. When you're employing hundreds of people, you feel like you've got no choice but to appear strong, even if you're crumbling inside. Your team's looking to you for inspiration and leadership. The last thing any business owner wants is for their team to start worrying that the MD's personal struggles could send the entire business to the wall. *M* was causing enough tension in the office, so I felt that I needed to remain calm and professional whenever I was talking to colleagues. They needed to know that there was still a business to run and we still not only had thriving businesses to service, but that everyone who retained our services expected world-class service. On top of that, trying to turn the business back onto a profitable track was more

## No Problem is Permanent

than just work to me: it was a matter of personal pride. That meant hiding how I really felt from almost all of my colleagues.

Men often perceive their professional success as a reflection of their success as a human being. I felt that if the business fell apart, then I had failed as a man. This made it even more difficult for me to reach out for help and support at the time. Whenever I did discuss my disagreements with and eventual divorce from *M* with anyone, that person was almost always a lawyer charging me £250 an hour for their time. You become a lot more conservative in expressing your feelings when each new thought is costing you £50. Worse still, the questions that the lawyers asked me just went over hugely traumatic arguments with *M* again, and again, and again.

"Mr Ansermoz, please tell us about what happened on *X* date at *X* O'Clock?" was a common request from them.

I needed building back up as a person, but their focus was purely on building a case to challenge *M*'s accusations in court. Can you imagine the anguish of fitting a detailed repetition of some of the saddest moments of your life into a busy 18-hour day of firefighting and saving your business from collapse? The emotional drain and exhaustion I suffered was horrific. I'm certain that the mental and physical toll that all this took on me made a major contribution to the health battles I would suffer a couple of years later.

Speaking to my family didn't improve the situation at all. Some of my relatives weren't fans of *M* to begin with and weren't shy about expressing their pleasure in what they saw as me (finally) realising that I'd made a huge mistake.

"It only took 10 years!" said an uncle. "We all knew she wasn't right for you…but you live and you learn. Cheer yourself up and have a pint."

Those words made the top 3 on the list of least helpful things that he possibly could have said. The truth was, I wasn't really living or learning. I felt trapped in a cycle of grief, guilt and depression with no obvious exit. My friends at the time weren't much help either.

Their usual response whenever I tried mentioning the situation was, "You'll get over it!"

I couldn't find a way to tell them that I needed much more from them emotionally. After all, depending on which group I hung out with, I was either aspiring to reach their level of business success or the successful one who'd built a growing business.

A blessing in disguise

Being the vulnerable one who was going through a prolonged traumatic experience wasn't an option in either group.

# Finding hope again...

During the day, I would sit in my office in my suit feeling just like I did when I was sitting in the pub all those years ago. If you're going through divorce while trying to keep your business on track, please don't suffer like I did. Find a friend who can empathise with what you're going through and talk to them about how you're feeling. You want someone who will actually listen to you and won't rush to judge how valid your feelings are or how improved your current situation would be if only you'd taken their advice in the first place. You also want to open up to someone who you know you can trust. Nowadays, many people will promise you their absolute discretion before telling their 3 closest mates everything that you've just told them. That's just wrong! You need to talk to someone who understands that you're asking for help and not for your struggles to become discussion points. Most importantly, you need someone who understands that the end of your marriage might yet end up in court and that things going round could actually damage your case costing you a fortune, and worse, ruining your reputation and good name too.

When you've found this person, you've got to be truly ready to accept their help and let your guard down. There's no point being reserved or defensive. If you don't get what you're feeling off your chest, then it will stay there with you.

In my case, there was only so long I could go on trying to hide how I felt. I was so worried about letting colleagues down that I constantly changed the subject asap when anybody asked how I felt. My colleague Gill had known for some time that I was far from my usual self and came up with a solution which would go on to change my life. She'd come across an influential American life and business coach called Tony Robbins after watching his videos online. *YouTube* was only just becoming a major global force, but his content was already on there. A passing interest developed into recommendations to everyone in the office after she had signed up to one of his courses. Tony was in a different league to other coaches. He emphasised taking action and turning doubt and low self-confidence into a plan to take back control of your life. I took the whole team down South for his next UK event,

No Problem is Permanent

which was in London. Going was really Gill's idea, but I said we'd all support her and go with her. I hoped that I would benefit hugely from his sessions too, but still didn't feel strong enough to let any of my colleagues know that.

Tony's event was called *UPW: Unleash the Power Within*. It left me feeling as free as a bird.

The event ran from Thursday to Monday and was jam-packed with sessions that showed everyone there how to master different aspects of their lives. From relationships to finance, everything was covered. Tony's sessions demanded that we all create goals and then hold ourselves accountable for achieving them. This wasn't just a case of writing a few goals down and hoping for the best. Tony was going around the room making sure that people made uncomfortable phone calls and let their families know on the spot about major life decisions that they'd been avoiding sharing. You never knew whether it would be your turn next, and I certainly didn't want to phone $M$ in front of a room full of people. I spent hours thinking about not just which goals I would action when I got home, but exactly how I would action them. Unfortunately, Gill was really the only other member of my team who had any interest in the sessions. On the way back from a quick break, I found my team hanging out in the lobby drinking coffee.

I wasn't happy and let them know about it:

"I've paid a fortune for us to be here to try to turn the business around, and you've spent the whole day chilling."

One of my colleagues, Jim, who was normally on it every day in the HR department summed up how many of them felt.

"Lloyd," he said, "My biggest goal is to dip this biscuit into my tea without it breaking. I've tried 10 times now and am slowly getting there. We just need them to unleash the sandwiches and then this will have been a productive few days off."

Everyone started laughing - apart from me.

# A new chapter...

As disappointed as I was, I understood that I couldn't force my team to take an interest in Tony's sessions, let alone appreciate the sessions as a crucial part of their self-development. Fortunately, Gill completely understood the value of what we'd spent the past few days doing.

## A blessing in disguise

"You know, you could sign up for Tony's Platinum Partnership Programme," she helpfully and very kindly suggested. "That gives you four events a year including the big one in Palm Springs. *Date with Destiny* changes people's lives. Nobody ever comes back the same. You need this, Lloyd. Leave all of the pain you've been carrying for so long on the other side of the ocean and build a different future for yourself when you come home. We're all in control of our own destiny. You just don't realise it yet because you're so upset about everything that's happening with *M.*"

I knew that she was right. It was the first time we'd really openly discussed how I was feeling and I realised that I didn't have to hide it anymore. I just had to solve the problems that were damaging my wellbeing and put a ton of effort into moving on with my life.

The programme cost £12,500, so my first question to Gill, who was our in-house bookkeeper, was, "Can the business afford it?"

She told me, "Yes, if we pay over 4 months it won't be too expensive now and will deliver you massive benefits for the rest of your life." That seemed like a deal I couldn't refuse.

"Thanks for understanding, Gill," I said with my biggest smile for a while. "Let's do this!"

Less than 10 minutes later I'd signed up and paid the first instalment. After experiencing just a few hours of Tony's Platinum programme, it was clear that this was the best investment I'd ever made.

After a few fascinating specialist sessions across the US, the big one came: *Date with Destiny*. I was full of nerves at the airport, ahead of boarding the flight from Gatwick to Houston and then flying on to Palm Springs. The prospect of a week talking about my deepest fears in a room full of hundreds of people made me feel a bit queasy. One shining light made everything easier though.

Despite everything I'd gone through, I'd managed to make an amazing decision even before attending *UPW*. I had met Naomi, who was and still is an absolute ray of sunshine in my life. She was the only person I called before boarding the plane.

"I know you can do this, Lloyd. It will be a tough week but so, so worth it. You'll feel so much better when you get home and I can't wait to give you a massive hug. Go out there and build the destiny you deserve!"

Then I got on the plane and never looked back.

## No Problem is Permanent

Unfortunately, however, I was left looking frantically at the departures board while sprinting through Houston Airport after my flight from Gatwick had landed. By the time I'd got through customs, collected my bag from the baggage carousel, and checked-in (again), my flight to Palm Springs had almost left. While cardio is important, I wasn't expecting to fit that much of it into such a short space of time. Miraculously, my tired body (which had already been travelling for 14 hours) slumped into my seat on the Palm Springs flight with just three minutes to spare. It felt like someone upstairs was even more determined to get me on that flight than I was.

Sadly, my bag didn't arrive with me in Palm Springs 3 hours later. It was still sitting somewhere in Houston Airport and wouldn't complete its journey to my Palm Springs resort for another 24 hours. Thankfully, the 'baggage claim' team at Palm Springs Airport couldn't have been more helpful if they'd tried. That generosity of spirit extended to a wonderful lady called Dorothy, whose clothing shop had closed when I arrived urgently looking for some nice clothes to wear until my bag arrived.

"Are you still open?" I asked while struggling to stay awake and trying my very best to hold in my frustration after what had been a hugely difficult 17 hours.

Some shop owners might have complained about my last-minute approach – not Dorothy.

"We're open for as long as you need," she reassured me with truly amazing kindness. She then even helped me to find a pair of trousers and two shirts. Dorothy's generosity didn't stop there either.

"Would you like me to steam your new shirts?" she gently enquired as I was preparing to dart off and leave her to lock-up.

"That would be amazing, thank you, but weren't you just locking-up? You've already gone above and beyond to help me."

Dorothy looked surprised, even shocked, at the suggestion that she would prioritise leaving work after a long day over doing everything in her power to make customers feel fantastic in their new clothes.

"You deserve to look your best in your new shirts. It's really no problem at all to give them a quick steam."

"Thank you so much, Dorothy, meeting you has been the highlight of my day!" was all I could say after that.

She nodded appreciatively, steamed my shirts and handed them back to me, beautifully boxed, just a few minutes later.

## A blessing in disguise

Imagine a high-street chain in the UK offering that level of service? They would have ushered me away the minute I turned up, doing nothing to help me manage a very difficult challenge. Instead, what could have been a crisis turned into a wonderful encounter and some lovely new clothes. Clearly no problem is permanent in Palm Springs.

The whole fortnight of events continued in that vein and was a series of incredible, life-changing experiences. The people, the noise and the intensity felt like something out of a film. Everyone was absolutely focused on each other's success. In a hall full of people, I was able to look at the people sitting around me, who I'd never met before, and know that they wanted me to win, and I wanted them to win too. We would regularly sing together too. The first of these songs was '*Sweet Caroline*'. The last time I'd sung that was with 90 blokes on an alcohol-fuelled weekend trip to Magaluf. In Spain, '*Sweet Caroline*' was our 'tour song'. If we weren't singing loudly enough, we hadn't got smashed enough that day. In Palm Springs, the contrast of singing the song as a symbol of our renewed lives, with our bodies full of faith and success rather than toxicity, was phenomenal and incredibly moving. The singing was also a perfect accompaniment to Tony's sessions.

The sessions mapped out exactly what each delegate's personal version of winning looked like. For me, it looked like getting new lawyers, getting my divorce sorted and finally, finally, building a new life for myself with Naomi. It also involved selling *Keen Kleen*. Peter had been back in contact with me for a few months now and there was only so long that I could afford to continue delaying getting a deal done with him.

This conclusion seemed so clear but had taken such a long and difficult journey to reach. Tony's sessions made the impossible seem not just an achievable goal but a set of easy decisions that I just hadn't seen yet. The *Date With Destiny* sessions were even more intense than the *UPW* ones.

The process of regularly writing down our destiny and plans for getting there involved going beyond difficult moments and breaking through the emotional barriers that were hindering our growth – in public. I realised that the sadness I was still feeling about the breakdown of my marriage to *M* was preventing me from fully focusing on anything else in life. I'd tried ignoring it, being angry about it and resenting it, but none of those reactions had brought me any happiness. I was still trapped in a depressing

## No Problem is Permanent

cycle almost three years after it had become obvious that our marriage was over. That was what made me accept that getting the divorce over as quickly as possible (rather than continuing to fight with *M*) would end the fights I was having with myself and help me to grow through the pain of the whole situation.

One of Tony's favourite life lessons to share, and the inspiration for this book's title, is:

"No problem is permanent."

Any and every challenge can be solved if you're willing to confront its root causes and do something to address them. Procrastination will kill you: sometimes literally if you're dealing with a major health challenge. Seeing a solution in every problem feels like such an easy and obvious answer to the challenges we all face, but that answer is so difficult to grasp. You can get so caught up in your emotional responses to people and events that you overlook the obvious solution that's right in front of you. Unfortunately for me, my focus on trying to relieve the mental health burden of what had now escalated into a multi-year divorce battle with *M* meant that I overlooked worrying physical health symptoms. The constant fatigue that I'd put down to work burnout turned out to be something devastatingly worse that almost cost me my life.

Those days in Palm Springs were magical. This special city is still one of the kindest and most thoughtful places I've ever visited. People instinctively would just say "Good morning" or "Have a nice day" on the regular walks I'd take during the retreat. Compare that to London, the setting for several of my meetings in the days before flying out of Gatwick. The UK's biggest city isn't its friendliest. Making eye contact with people in the street there, let alone saying "Hello" to them, is almost considered a crime. Things couldn't have been more different in Palm Springs and I was loving every minute of it.

That being said, I missed Naomi and Holly so much while I was away and hugely appreciated the wonderful surprise that I received when my bag finally arrived from Houston a day into the trip. While rummaging through my stuff, I found Holly's little toy monkey, Scruffy, carrying a lovely note from Naomi. That was such a thoughtful thing for Naomi to do and made me more determined than ever to return to them as a better person following my *Date with Destiny*. Holly must have missed Scruffy while he enjoyed a week's holiday in America, but hopefully she felt better knowing that he was making her Daddy very happy.

## A blessing in disguise

Eventually, it was time to board my flight home, carrying a new lease on life - as well as some of the very healthy food and recipes we'd spent the week experiencing - back with me. Who knew that drinking wheatgrass would actually make me feel healthier and more prepared than ever to tackle life's challenges. First on my list of challenges to knock on the head was the legal nightmare that was draining me of everything I had and had also been putting *Keen Kleen's* future at serious risk.

Almost as soon as my flight home landed, I phoned Fergal's colleague, Kevin. He was the lawyer I wanted to represent me against *M*'s team, but because his firm acted for *Keen Kleen*, he hadn't been able to act for me personally in this case due to a conflict of interest - until now. Kevin had just moved to a leading firm in Worcester. The city whose cathedral had marked a major chapter of my business journey was about to play a huge part in my next chapter. I finally had access to the lawyer I wanted. His expert advice was needed urgently. *M* had already secured an order of nearly £500k against me and was coming after more. She wanted everything I had and her legal team was determined to take it for her. At this point, it would have been very easy for me to fight back aggressively.

However, Tony's sessions had shown me that another approach would be far more lucrative (and make me far happier in the long-term). It's difficult to emphasise how much your peace of mind is worth. Kevin saved me by getting rid of *M*'s case while protecting my cash flow.

When I met him for the first time in his new Worcester office, he said "Here's what we're going to do, Lloyd. Firstly, we'll cut down that hugely excessive order she secured against you. You haven't got the remaining £250k in cash, so I'll tell the judge that the order was overvalued and she's getting £50k or nothing." Then the genius part came.

"You'll pay off that £50k quarterly over 12 months. Then it's over. You can move on with your life and she'll have to move on with hers too."

That sounded wonderful, Kevin represented me outstandingly in court, and, finally, after more years than I'd like to remember, my divorce from *M* was finalised.

It was over.

All the pain was over and I could finally build a new future with Naomi. The constant pain and drama of the past few years had become history in just a few months. A huge weight had been

## No Problem is Permanent

lifted from my shoulders and I felt as free as a bird. The only way was up, even if that journey would be slightly bumpier than I'd originally expected.

The undisclosed sale price and £150k annual salary that I negotiated with Peter in return for all of *Keen Kleen's* remaining contracts felt like peanuts. The business could have been worth so much more than that. Without all of the drama, *Keen Kleen* would have continued turning over millions annually, even allowing for the loss of a few key accounts. But, the money Peter offered was enough for me to get rid of my nightmare divorce case and provide a comfortable life for my new family. While all of this was going on, Naomi and I welcomed our wonderful daughter, Holly, into the world. We decided to relocate to Cheshire to make those long drives to Warrington things of the past. Then we started house hunting in search of what we hoped would be our happily ever after.

While the end of my divorce was finally in sight, and *Keen Kleen's* sale approached completion, the beginning of a completely new challenge was just around the corner. My will to overcome any and all adversity would be tested like never before. But, hey, no problem is permanent...

The fatigue which felt like I hadn't slept in weeks was getting worse and worse. Almost weekly, normal tasks were leaving me completely shattered. I often ended up conked out on the sofa (or worse) in my car for absolutely no reason. On the scariest occasion, my car sped down the motorway at 90mph with me slumped completely unconscious in the driver's seat with no idea what was going on. To this day, I still have absolutely no idea how I survived and was so relieved not to have hurt anyone. Perhaps someone upstairs was looking after me. I needed them a few more times after that.

Naomi had mentioned getting my symptoms checked out a few times, but I'd always explained them away as "No big deal."

"Thankfully it's nothing to worry about," said the GP during the appointment I eventually booked. "You've just been worn out with work; particularly given your recent extensive travel to and from Warrington. You're also showing symptoms of depression, which is consistent with everything you've been going through personally of late. Take these tablets, they'll help you to sleep better and give you more energy during the day. Then, I'm confident that these bouts of severe fatigue will end, and you won't need further treatment."

## A blessing in disguise

That was it.

Of course, it's hugely important that anyone feeling depressed seeks any help, support and treatment that they need. But I was convinced that something was seriously wrong with my physical health too…

# Chapter Nine

## A blessing in disguise

"It can't just be depression Naomi. I can't ever remember feeling this ill." Sitting with her one morning, we were both urgently trying to work out what was causing my symptoms, worried that something much worse than what the GP had suggested might be behind them.

Then one evening, just before we'd completed the move to Warrington, everything went dark, and my life changed forever.

As I was putting Holly to bed, my head smashed against the floor. I collapsed and had no idea where I was. Naomi's presence as she walked into the room didn't even register with me. I was unconscious, fitting and barely breathing. Naomi phoned 999 and suddenly our home was full of paramedics. As sirens blared, blue lights flashed and medical experts rushed around carrying out almost every test imaginable, death felt like it had sucked my body into a horrible cloud of darkness.

As the ambulance rushed to A&E, tomorrow started slipping through my fingers.

A blessing in disguise

Fitting, being blue-lighted and feeling so ill that Naomi was terrified she wouldn't see me again had to be down to more than work pressures. Those pills from the GP went straight in the bin and I decided never to put my health last again. If I'd applied Tony Robbins' lessons to my health as well as other aspects of my life, perhaps things might have panned out differently. As already mentioned though, Captain Hindsight needs an urgent performance improvement plan to address his timing. A call to the surgery...

"That must have been a deeply shocking experience," said the GP, referring to my recent A&E visit. "However, thankfully it's nothing to worry about. You've just been worn out with work; particularly given your recent extensive travel to and from Warrington. You're also showing symptoms of depression, which is consistent with everything you've been going through personally of late. Take these tablets, they'll help you to sleep better and give you more energy during the day. Then, I'm confident that these bouts of severe fatigue will end, and you won't need further treatment."

That was it.

Of course, it's hugely important that anyone feeling depressed seeks any help, support and treatment that they need. But I was convinced that something was seriously wrong with my physical health too. Fitting, being blue-lighted and feeling so ill that Naomi was terrified she wouldn't see me again had to be down to more than work pressures. The staff at A&E did their absolute best to ensure that I woke up after that ambulance journey, and that my heart kept ticking. There are only so many tests that they can do though. After this GP appointment about a week later, I took the tablets home, still completely unconvinced. Instead of taking them the following Monday, those pills went straight in the bin. A call to the surgery followed asking for an urgent referral. It was then that they told me that the *NHS* had a 9-month waiting list to see a consultant neurologist. There was no way I was waiting 9 months. That was just impossible.

After careful research, I used my health insurance to book an appointment privately with the highly respected neurologist, Professor Shepherd. As soon as I walked into the Prof's office, it was obvious that he suspected my symptoms were down to far more than just burnout.

After reprising everything that had happened, he asked:
"Lloyd, please could you walk across the room for me?" I did.

No Problem is Permanent

"And back again? Thank you, please sit down. Are you happy for us to take some x-rays, just to rule the worst out."

The penny still hadn't quite dropped as to what the worst could be. I thought things were bad but could never have imagined how serious my situation was. Despite struggling to walk straight across the Professor's office, I left hoping for the best and went straight back to work. That was my way of dealing with things at the time. Like many entrepreneurs, throwing myself into my work provided a welcome distraction from other things that were happening in my life.

I'd let Peter know that I was seeing Prof Shepherd that day and he gave me a call when I got home.

He kindly asked:

"How are you feeling Lloyd? We've got a huge meeting next to *Bolton Football Club's Reebok Stadium* on Thursday and I wanted to check that you were OK to attend. If not, it's no problem, we can easily find someone to cover. Your health is the most important thing."

"Thanks so much for calling, Peter, everything's OK. I look forward to seeing you on Thursday," I said, completely overlooking the reality of the situation.

I should never have attended that meeting but, at the time, *Bolton* were a *Premier League* club. Their top-flight presence made the area surrounding their stadium a hub for top-flight businesses. The deal on the table would net huge revenue for *Indepth* and significantly boost my annual bonus too. There I was again, putting work ahead of my health. Of course, your work is hugely important, but it's never more important than your life. No meeting is worth reducing your life expectancy and losing years of time with your loved ones later in life. Nowadays, I urge all of my mentees to put their health first at all times. If only I'd taken my own advice back then. Captain Hindsight is making a frustrating number of appearances in this book!

# Awful diagnoses aren't always the end of the road...

So that Thursday's meeting happened, went well and everything seemed fine until I got back into the car. The time was 2pm

A blessing in disguise

exactly, and the phone rang just before I set off on another long drive home - our family's move to Cheshire couldn't come soon enough. It was Prof Shepherd's secretary who first indicated that something was seriously wrong. She phoned and said, "Mr Ansermoz we would like you to come in for some further tests. We've booked you an urgent appointment for tomorrow. If this is not convenient, please let us know."

There was no way I could get back from Bolton overnight so asked if an appointment the day after, that Saturday, would be possible. The Professor's secretary rang back within 10 minutes and confirmed my appointment in two days' time. Then I knew that something was seriously wrong. As soon as I'd sat down in Prof Shepherd's office that Saturday, he showed me just how serious the situation was.

He flashed my X-Rays up on the screen and said, "Sadly, your x-rays showed a large cyst in your cerebellum. If you don't take action immediately, then your life is in serious danger."

"So, we've got to do something right now?" I asked as my initial shock developed into a growing realisation of the situation I was facing.

"Yes, indeed we must," said Prof Shepherd in a voice that was sad but relieved that I understood and accepted the gravity of the situation. "I'm referring you to my colleague Professor Cruickshank, who will see you on Tuesday. He is one of the leading neurosurgeons in the country and will be able to carry out the operation that will give you the best possible chances of survival."

It was then that he diagnosed the cyst as a medulloblastoma. It was the size of a large peach. Nobody in his office was calling it cancer for fear of upsetting me, but I've always called things as they are.

That's why, when I first met Prof Cruickshank and he referred to my diagnosed medulloblastoma, I asked "Can we just call it cancer? That's what it is."

"OK, I regret to tell you that your cancer is even more malignant than your X-rays showed-" was Prof Cruickshank's sombre reply. "Your only chance of surviving this is if my team performs an emergency 8 and-a-half hour operation to remove your tumour a week on Saturday. You'll need to attend hospital from next Saturday and you will also need to be admitted to intensive care immediately following your operation and for four days thereafter. Then you can return to your hospital room. Without surgery, you may not survive the fortnight."

Nothing could have prepared me (or Naomi) for that.

The pure fear that consumed every part of me remains difficult to put into words. We just sat in the car with Holly, who was only 2 at the time, completely lost for words.

Every entrepreneur will feel dread in the pit of their stomach at some point during their lives, but nothing comes close to that. Either you have an enormously difficult surgery which will take months to recover from and may not leave you the same, or your life ends in a fortnight. Going through with the surgery was my only option - I needed to be there for Naomi, Holly and Ian. Even if surgery leaves you weaker physically, as long as you're still breathing, you can still positively impact the world. Crushing setbacks only transform into the biggest blessings if you keep trying to move forwards.

After a lengthy pause before driving home, Naomi and I decided that the only way forwards was to put all of our trust into Prof Cruickshank and his team. That was the best chance we had of making it through this. Sometimes life gives you lemons but on other occasions, it gives you cancer. You have to accept cancer to fight it. If you spend all your time and energy fighting the diagnosis, then you'll use up valuable resources that you need to pull through surgery and overcome chemo. Don't wait for crucial treatment either.

If you can take out private health insurance, secure a policy as soon as possible. You never know when convenient appointments and extra options for consultations and surgery that this insurance gives you could quite literally be the difference between life and death. Without private health insurance, we would have been left completely stranded. Instead, I secured that vital consultation and follow-up with Prof Shepherd, and then the life-saving urgent appointment and surgery with Prof Cruickshank.

After spending the Sunday processing everything that the previous day had thrown at us, Naomi phoned the team at *Indepth* and let them know that I would be off sick for some time. Then, in the days before I was scheduled to go into hospital, we sat down with my parents and siblings to tell them the news.

That was so hard. Everyone reacted differently: tears, worry and pure shock that what I'd initially put down to fatigue was potentially terminal cancer were understandable initial reactions. Then something wonderful happened.

## A blessing in disguise

As we discussed the situation and my treatment plan for hours, those negative feelings turned into a strong resolve to beat this cancer as a family and get back to normal life as quickly as possible. A cancer diagnosis doesn't just impact you; it impacts everyone around you and you all need each other to find paths forwards. This strength and support were the two most important things that I took with me into a long stay in hospital.

Through the operation, 4 days in intensive care and then a week in my room, I was alone for almost two weeks. This gave me time to focus on the many inspirational and motivating teachings which Prof Cruickshank's team had allowed Naomi to stick all over the walls of the room before I got there. These teachings gave me the confidence to believe that even when I felt at death's door, a bright future lay ahead of me. Some of the most notable were from leading thinker, Deepak Chopra.

'All great changes are preceded by chaos', seemed like an accurate assessment of my situation. Finding a positive future to look forward to after the surgery was key to getting through it. Worrying about potential risks of surgery and letting concern over life expectancy weigh me down wouldn't do anyone any good - least of all me. If you're currently facing a major health challenge, focus on what you can still do as well as ever. Everyone has strengths, even when an horrific illness leaves them so weak that they can't get themselves out of bed. Imagine feeling as free as a bird and then having your wings clipped, quite literally, by a terminal diagnosis.

Even after surgery, I wasn't guaranteed to see the end of the year, let alone Holly's first day of school. It would have been easy to just give up and resign myself to death. But what growth has negativity ever achieved? Sometimes the best way to fight is to let go of the fear, pain and sadness that you're feeling, accept adversity as a part of life and decide to keep going and build from there.

'When you make a choice, you change the future', seemed more than appropriate too. You always have a choice, even if the world feels like it's stacked against you. Even if you're sitting in a hospital bed and can't go anywhere, you can still choose to perceive the world positively. You can choose to respond to the team looking after you in a kind and friendly manner. You can choose to be grateful that you have access to the very latest in innovative healthcare. Nothing makes you appreciate life more than almost losing it.

## No Problem is Permanent

I should never have attended that meeting near the *Reebok* and was determined to put my health first at all times from the minute I was allowed to leave the hospital.

As I was preparing to come home, I couldn't help thinking about one of the most inspirational speakers that we had the privilege of hearing during the Palm Springs sessions. His remarks were incredibly personal, so I won't use his name here. Let's call him 'Brian'. Brian's life had been turned upside down by a car accident when he was just 17 years old. The accident broke Brian's neck but never broke his spirit. Doctors had told Brian that his injuries from the accident would leave him unable to ever use a wheelchair, drive or do anything without other people's assistance again.

Apparently, he would never enjoy independence again, and yet, here he was, wheeling himself onto stage and telling us all his story. Even more impressively, Brian was truly grateful not just for his life, but for the accident which seemed to have taken so much from him. What would have been a defining tragedy of other people's lives had given Brian a completely new lease on life. Now he felt inspired to change as many lives as possible by achieving things that were, apparently, impossible, and then encouraging others to do the same. This wasn't Brian's only booking of the day. By that point, he was a renowned public speaker and in demand across America. If he could embrace his medical diagnosis as a blessing in disguise, then surely I could too.

Tony Robbins' "No problem is permanent" quote (which had also inspired Brian) took on a new meaning from that moment on. If I could get through this, I could get through anything. However, as I spent hour after hour alone in my hospital room, it became obvious that something on top of wonderful support from my family and friends was helping me to survive through this illness. My faith in God had all but disappeared during my adult life, but it came back then. This faith would be key to recovering and rebuilding my life too. Sadly, it had been absent from my life for far too long.

When I was working at the bakery, the most important thing in life seemed to be the opportunities that you create for yourself. I didn't feel like a higher power was going to help me to better my lifestyle. The only way to improve life for myself and my family seemed to be to spend more time working than praying. In a world of long hours and low wages, there didn't seem to be anyone looking out for us apart from each other.

A blessing in disguise

When the life I'd been building with Tracey fell apart, again it seemed as though I was on my own, just trying to get through each day without facing some new drama, without a long-term purpose. I remember sitting in the pub back then and thinking:
"If there is a God, why would he want me feeling this sad all the time?"

Again, getting myself out of that negative situation seemed to be solely my responsibility. I didn't feel as though faith would make any difference to my outcomes. The teaching of 'love thy neighbour' significantly declined in meaning when many of those I worked alongside seemed to resent my success despite my encouraging theirs. Instead of celebrations of new projects secured to support the *Dairy Crest* team, returns to the office would suddenly turn into one of those rowdy market film scenes where everyone was haggling over how much effort they'd put into securing the deal and why they deserved a bigger bonus. I did it too.

"That's 50% I've increased revenue by in the last 6 months!" I made clear after a particularly productive meeting with *Dairy Crest*'s managers.

I was all for encouraging others, but at the time, I felt like I needed to come first in everything. Part of that probably came from seeking validation from my parents. The result was constantly feeling a sale away from a reward that never came. The idea that faith might provide me with the validation I'd been searching for so long seemed alien. My purpose seemed to be to prove to those around me that I could run a successful business. Thinking of successful business-building as something more meaningful than generating revenue didn't occur to me until the friends and partners I met after incorporating *Keen Kleen* helped me to view the world through a different lens.

Even then, purpose didn't seem like a product of faith. It seemed like something which I could set out in business plans, staff handbooks and onboarding policies. Fulfilling this purpose seemed like a natural part of growth: helping an ever-growing team build fulfilling careers and lives for themselves. If someone had asked me what the inspiration behind this purpose-based strategy was, I would have shown them one of the fascinating business strategy books rapidly filling my shelves at that time - not a religious one. There were none of them to be seen on my bookshelves. I felt as if I was in control of everything happening around me and didn't need God. From deep cleaning cellars to employing 230 people and buying buildings, it felt like everything I touched turned to gold - until that gold almost completely dissolved.

## Faith is never lost forever...

Even in the darkest moments of my divorce from *M*, I still had some ability to influence the outcome of events as they unfolded. But as I sat in Professor Cruickshank's office and heard him spell out just how close to death I was, any feeling of control completely evaporated. That was probably where that immense feeling of fear came from - not knowing what would happen or what I could do to improve things. After years of defining my life through business deals, it became clear that any extension of my life would have to be powered by faith. While the medical mastery of the Professors and their teams kept me breathing, I needed to live spiritually too.

The first step on this new journey involved changing my thought process to accept everyone without judgement until proven otherwise. There's nothing like being in intensive care and quite literally unable to do anything for yourself to make you appreciate everybody around you. I felt as though someone upstairs was trying to tell me something.

The first part of my life had been all about Lloyd. This was different. Now my focus was on growing through helping others - not for my own gain but primarily for theirs. This wasn't about me being a successful business leader. It was about putting others first in everything.

The next key step was to avoid negativity. Surrounding myself with love would be the new order of the day. Nothing gives those "Life's too short" remarks meaning like being at death's door.

How often have you heard someone make a negative comment about another person? How often have you made those comments? If you add up all of the time that you've spent criticising others or hearing this criticism, how long have you wasted in a cycle of negativity? What else could you have achieved in that time?

We're all on this earth for a short time and we can all choose how we spend those years. Be someone who spreads happiness and aims not just for a Happiness-Centred Business, but a happiness-centred life. That was the person that I needed to become after recovering from my surgery.

A blessing in disguise

The third step involved establishing faith in people as well as a higher power. It's all too easy to discount someone's opinion or ignore them because of biases that you didn't even know you had. Maintaining faith in people until they give you a reason not to sounds simple but is actually incredibly tough. You have to say 'yes' far more than you say 'no'. You have to give people a chance when your instinct might be to politely avoid them. Looks genuinely can be deceiving and the best business partner is not always the most suited and booted person in the room. You have to put your assumptions to one side, listen far more than you talk and accept the fact that the answer you'd convinced yourself would grow your business could actually be the wrong one. Faith is essential if you want push through conventional cultural boundaries and embrace something brilliantly different. It played an essential role in my life from then on.

So that was my deal with God.

Embracing living for others rather than living for myself would see me go home from hospital. Faith adds more value to your life than anything you could possibly buy - it's not dependent on religion though. While I'm now a practising Christian, many ethical principles around treating people fairly and with respect can be applied without reference to any particular religion's teachings. You don't need to attend a place of worship every week to be a good person. You just need to appreciate the good in others.

As it happened, I left the hospital far earlier than I should have done. The surgery had, miraculously, been a complete success. Over more than 8 hours, Professor Cruickshank had removed 99.9% of the peach that had been weighing down my life expectancy. What followed was a shattering course of chemotherapy. Thankfully, Peter fully appreciated how tough this would be. A few days after I got home, we spoke on the phone.

"Lloyd," he said, "Don't even think about coming back to work. I'll pay you your basic salary until you're back to full health, so you won't need to worry about bills. Just focus on getting better. We need you at your best and that means we need you to beat this cancer."

While I hugely appreciated his generosity, missing out on bonuses that I would normally hit easily was frustrating - especially because *M* made no account of the change to my earnings in what I had to fork out every quarter to pay her off. But, hey, what would have previously massively frustrated me was

## No Problem is Permanent

now just an inconvenience. I was back at home with Naomi and Holly, and we wouldn't have to worry about money. We could focus on enjoying time with each other that was so nearly taken from us. Their love and support during this time was invaluable. There were so many times when I doubted if I would completely recover and Naomi always motivated me to keep fighting the last bit of this tumour and get back to full health.

She would always say:

"You know how good you are at your job, with your new perspective you can be even better. I'm sure you can eventually build another business that will employ almost double the number of people that *Keen Kleen* ever did and generate life-changing rewards for the whole team - not just us. Imagine how many people you can help to retire early and live their dream lives. Then, you'll be free from all of the pain of the last few years and we can move on into something more wonderful than either of us could have ever imagined."

That kept me going. As the months wore on though, my frustrations at not being able to work became harder and harder to suppress. This was well before the era of fully tech-enabled home offices where you can log-on and get yourself straight back into the thick of it in just a few clicks. I was sitting at home every day, not having any contact with work, feeling like climbing the walls but missing the physical strength to even do that. When you've spent so many years having to do a million things a day without fully ticking off your to-do-list, doing nothing goes against every fibre of your being. The last place you ever want to be is on your settee. Naomi was amazing throughout that whole year. The only times I ever went out was to get chemotherapy or radiotherapy. Chemo is the worst. It just saps all of your energy out of you. You've literally got nothing left and basic tasks like making yourself a sandwich feel like climbing Mount Everest. When you're not asleep, you're feeling like you've picked up a version of COVID-19 which is 100 times stronger and hasn't been discovered yet. In those few moments where you feel a little bit closer to your normal self, absolutely everything winds you up. My weight went up to 16.5 stone from 13 stone over the course of this treatment.

When you don't look or feel the same as the business leader whose life was turned upside down by a cancer diagnosis, your support system is key to restoring some of your self-esteem. If you

A blessing in disguise

know a business owner who's had one of those diagnoses, give them a call.

It will mean the world to them.

Too often, people hope that someone else will reach out to someone they know, who will then feel better. The hoped for connection doesn't happen and the recovering entrepreneur doesn't get the help they were looking for. Saying that you'll be there for people and then actually being there are two completely different things. If you're thinking of reaching out to a friend, just do it. You never know if the worst-case scenario might happen and you might lose them while you put off phoning them.

I owe so much to my closest friends at the time and Naomi. Without their endless support, I might just have given up on my career completely. Their motivation inspired me to keep getting back up, getting treated and carrying on with my career. Remember to be kind to the people who pull you through times like this. The last thing you want to do is to give them flak because of something else that's bothering you. Sadly, that can so often happen though and it's a testament to how wonderful they are as people that they stick with you through all that.

# Sometimes that fairytale return doesn't happen…

Although it took 5 years to get fully cleared of brain cancer, I was able to return to work after that first year of treatment had finished. Peter had been generous in continuing to pay me my basic salary while I'd been off, so I was determined to return to *Indepth* and sustain the growth that had fallen through our fingertips during my first stint there.

I still remember something Naomi said to me before I headed out to the office on my first day back.

"Why don't you just set up your next business now? Why are you going back? You know how much value you've created over all these years. No employer is ever going to pay you what you're truly worth. Surely, after everything you've been through, now is the perfect time to start something new."

The truth was that I needed to spend some time working for someone else before even thinking about launching another business. I was still a long way off 100% in my health or my income. On top of all that, the thought of working the hours that a new business demands seemed a bridge too far. It seemed more sensible to help *Indepth* reach ambitious new growth targets rather than to try and achieve that growth with a startup from scratch.

More than anything else, I genuinely hoped that things would be different when I returned to Head Office in Warrington. The opportunity to take everything I'd learnt from *Keen Kleen* and use it to support Peter, who had given me such an amazing break all those years ago and been such a support throughout my surgery, felt like one of the moments in life where everything comes full circle. My hope on going back to *Indepth* was that I wouldn't need to set up another one of my own businesses. That hope proved to be immensely short-lived. After that horrible encounter with Geoff over Paddi's book, it became obvious that Peter and his wider team didn't want my help in the way that I'd hoped.

I can still picture myself sitting in Peter's office when it became obvious that professionally we'd reached a point of no return.

"Lloyd, colleagues have raised serious concerns about your conduct," he told me without batting an eyelid. "We need to part company immediately and permanently. This gives me no pleasure as I've liked and respected you for many years. However, I think we both know that we've reached a point of no return."

He was right about one thing. There was no way that I could stay at *Indepth* but he was wrong about another – there was no way that I was leaving without the money I was due. Peter knew that the business couldn't afford to pay me what I needed anymore, and the allegations of misconduct were spurious attempts to lower the figure that he would need to pay to get me out of the business. "OK," I replied, "But I gave you a business with a multi-million-pound turnover in a hugely cut-price deal and I'll need every penny that I'm owed."

Silence followed before Peter's secretary knocked on the door and said, "Sorry to interrupt, Mr Roach, I just wanted to let you know that you'll need to set-off for your flight from Manchester in about ten minutes." He thanked her before we wrapped up.

Our conversation resumed a few days later over the phone. I called Peter and let him know exactly how much I was owed and that, sadly, I would be forced to take legal action if he refused to pay me that amount. I'm hugely pleased that this legal action wasn't necessary as I still respected him hugely and remained grateful for the trust he and Jackie had placed in me. We had a few

A blessing in disguise

much calmer meetings after that and hammered out a deal that allowed me to walk away with enough compensation to see Naomi, Holly and myself through for 18 months or so. Peter agreed to a payment schedule that worked for both of us and allowed us both to move on. Sometimes in business you can easily find yourself at odds with your friends. It's crucial to remember that negotiations are just business and not allow them to damage your respect for each other.

While all this was going on, I had another encounter with Geoff in the office. While it would be a long stretch to describe this conversation as happy, it did help me to add more colour to my thinking about how the industry needed to change. "Which cleaners do we have on today?" began Geoff.

"We really should call them operatives," I insisted. "They have key skills that this business depends on. Calling them 'cleaners' is highly disrespectful as it fails to acknowledge everything that's involved in keeping professional environments pleasant and well-maintained."

"So *as I was saying...*" he continued with almost artisanal sarcasm, "Cleaners...!"

"Really, Geoff...?" I sighed quite loudly. "Are you really going to keep referring to vital professionals like we're on the set of some awful TV show from the 60's? Times change and operatives are looking for far more from the companies they work for. Clients are looking for more complex and personalised services crystallised in long-term partnerships. Office teams want to feel special. If we don't get on top of this now, others will. Then they'll leave us behind. If you want to this business to keep making serious money for another 40 years, you need to change before the industry forces you to."

Fortunately, that time, he just huffed and I left the room without me needing to quickly duck any books, magazines or newspapers. Knowing that a few days later, I would be beginning a new chapter of my life made all the difference. I dwelt much less on that encounter than I had on our previous one.

For the first time in a long time, I had time, money and good health all in the same place, at the same time. Despite my latest difficult departure from *Indepth*, life seemed fairly rosy. It felt as though the time had come to launch another business. After the wonderful success that *Keen Kleen* had enjoyed over those first few years, a drama-free version of *Keen Kleen* with better company culture and "World Class" client service seemed sure to change many people's lives forever.

I couldn't just keep my ideas for what the Happiness-Centred Business could achieve, and how it could change the cleaning industry in my head. A ten-year plan for this new business followed. Within 10 years, it would sell, netting me a £multi-million sum and leaving much more to be shared between our leadership team. The core team would all receive equity in the business, ensuring that they were rewarded for their loyalty, dedication and passion for excellence. Lives would change and more importantly, clients wouldn't just receive maintenance services. They would enjoy the world-class managed services they deserved. These services would far exceed what had been normal for so many years in the facilities management sector.

My aim for this new business wasn't just to look after sites and the hardware that made them tick. It was to offer a premium concierge service which allowed businesses to solve any cleaning or maintenance issues in a quick call to our team. 'Managed services' just gives a completely different impression to the 'facilities management' or 'FM' labels which are often stuck on the cleaning industry. FM is a radio frequency; we would be helping connect dots at the heart of businesses nationwide. While many businesses at the time and previously had offered managed services, nobody was offering the complete wraparound client care that we would offer. Finding the perfect branding for the new business that reflected this important difference was absolutely crucial.

# What's in a name?...

This new business needed a Brand that symbolised the trust that sat at the core of both our team's relationships with each other and our relationships with clients. In fact, the people who invested in our services would be more than just 'clients'. They would be partners. Our wider team, whether they were office-based staff or site-based operatives, would blend seamlessly into our partners' teams to deliver a level of service beyond anything they had experienced before. Nothing would ever be too much trouble. Most importantly, our partners would (eventually) all agree to give our operatives the respect that their skills deserved and never, ever dismiss them as 'cleaners'. Our operatives could trust us to

## A blessing in disguise

look after them and celebrate their talents as much as we could trust them to impress our partners with incredible work. The name that summed all of that trust up was *'Fidelis'*, literally 'Honest, loyal friend' in Latin.

Why not use an English word?

Because doing what everybody else does won't get anyone anywhere.

In an industry where names aren't memorable and often get mixed-up, choosing something that stood out was the only way to go. Choosing a name that really means something to people matters too. So many business owners do what I did with *Keen Kleen* – pick a founder or a loved one's name or surname and put it together with what the business does (maybe with some alliteration). The new beginning that *Fidelis* symbolised needed to express values that went well beyond just me. This wasn't just about me. It was about trying to inspire cultural change across the industry. Creating a profitable managed services business has never been easy but is achievable with good commercial planning and hard work. The real challenge is in creating a business which is both profitable and Happiness-Centred. That's why this new company's name had to say more than: "We're here to make as much money as possible." The name had to instantly demonstrate our commitment to doing things in the right way and leaving much more of a legacy than just cash. That's why leading with trust in everything we did, including the *Fidelis* branding was so important.

If you're considering starting a new business or changing your company's name, think about what values you want your business to be known for and go from there. What's the first thing that you want to pop into people's minds when they see your brand? If you don't define your business, then others will define it for you. That might not always be in the way you were hoping for. Standing for something is the best way to stand apart from your competitors and grow a business that produces much more than just financial goodness.

So...off I went to create this new mix of profitability and joy. To make things even better, Naomi and I welcomed our wonderful son Oliver into the world a few months before launching *Fidelis*. Life felt like it couldn't be going better. Naomi, Holly, Oliver and I moved back to the Midlands, finding a lovely house in the charming village of Hints, near Tamworth. Setting *Fidelis* up was a very smooth process and thanks to our current investment

## No Problem is Permanent

returns, we didn't have to take a wage from the business for some time. That meant that 100% of the early revenue that came in could be re-invested to grow *Fidelis*. The aim was to surpass even the most memorable successes I'd enjoyed with *Keen Kleen*. Great professional people working alongside us powered this growth forwards and we began to pick up some very lucrative contracts. Industry people started talking about *Fidelis* too. They were impressed by our early work and the business gained traction before any of us had even considered advertising on social media.

I felt on top of the world again after leaving a particularly exciting onboarding meeting with an impressive new client. There was a short break before a special team celebration to mark the occasion. None of us thought that anything could push us off this new, positive track towards a happy and growing business.

But then, a very challenging moment threatened everything…

# Chapter Ten

## It's just what we do around here

"Has anyone seen my phone?"

In a flash, my thoughts had switched from celebrating *Fidelis'* growing achievements to getting a hold of the GP as quickly as possible. I'd gone for a pee but all that had come out was blood. It turned the toilet bowl a shade of red that will stay with me forever. Nothing can prepare you for that kind of shock.

One of my colleagues sensed that something was wrong from how long I spent in the loo. As soon as I asked for it, she gave me my phone but I didn't actual book an emergency appointment straight away. Instead, I got distracted by an incoming call. People deal with shock in different ways and that was how I responded to that crushing feeling at the time. Only after speaking to Naomi once the work call had finished did I make the call I should have made about an hour beforehand. As usual, Naomi promised to support me through whatever came next. Tests followed a few days later. I hoped for the best as optimism had been in the air lately. Things genuinely seemed like they were turning a corner.

No Problem is Permanent

Maybe my symptoms had been caused by a freak injury or a condition that was quickly and easily treatable.

The GP called the day after my appointment. It wasn't good news.

"Mr Ansermoz, I regret to inform you that your symptoms may be related to cancer. An appointment has been arranged for you immediately at our specialist medical centre in Burton for further tests to confirm diagnosis."

I received the news I'd been dreading at that appointment.

"Mr Ansermoz, as you can see from the thorough examination carried out in your presence, you have 3 tumours within your bladder. You require surgery immediately."

Further investigation showed that these were all grade 4 tumours – the most aggressive type. Yet again, I'd gone from feeling mildly unwell to seeing my whole life hanging in the balance. It would be easy to completely lose hope after this diagnosis. However, when Naomi and I were given the news, I knew that hope lived and, better still, she shared life with me every day. We resolved to fight this cancer just as hard as we'd fought the brain tumour. I would look to begin treatment immediately and do everything possible to get through to the other side of this and carry on with our life.

The problem was that a further specialist appointment to discuss this surgery was scheduled far from immediately. It would be 12 weeks before I could see a specialist on the *NHS*. In that time, the disease might spread so badly that I would risk losing my bladder altogether, or worse, losing my life. Apart from dying, losing my bladder was one of the worst things in life that I could think of. My life would never be the same again if that happened. Having to wear an urostomy bag at the football, in business meetings and when relaxing with my family felt unthinkable. I'd been through a lot, but that felt like a bridge too far. Those who wear these bags and carry on with their everyday lives impress me every day. I don't know how they manage. Thankfully, the private health insurance I'd held onto saved both my bladder (by a matter of millimetres) and my life.

As we were driving back from Burton, Naomi made a brilliant suggestion. "You've still got your insurance, so why don't we phone Prof Cruickshank and ask if he can refer you to a private specialist for a consultation and surgery as soon as possible?" Minutes later, we pulled over and she made the call.

It's just what we do around here

"Naomi," Prof Cruickshank said in a concerned but reassuring voice. "I'm so glad that you called. This is one of the most severe diagnoses of bladder cancer that a person can receive. Lloyd hasn't got three weeks, in fact, he needed emergency surgery three weeks **ago**. I'm referring you to my colleague, Dr Syed, who is one of the UK's most experienced and respected urologists. I'm sorry to tell you that this process will be even tougher than the treatment we gave Lloyd to remove his brain tumour. I'm confident that Lloyd will pull through though. He always does."

The only reply that felt appropriate was "Thank you so much 'Prof'. I hope you've saved his life again."

Dr Syed's response was phenomenal. He phoned me within hours of my conversation with the 'Prof' and three days later, I was back on the operating table. Thankfully, the four operations (which all involved taking out part of my bladder) were eventually successful, but they took so much out of me. Then came the question of whether to carry out further surgery to completely remove the cancer, at the risk of removing my bladder entirely. Dr Syed was hesitant to carry out further surgery for exactly that reason.

Things got to a point where he told me, "Sadly, there's not much more we can shave off. Any more and you might lose your bladder without eliminating all presence of cancer."

On the other hand, there was also a significant risk that if any of the cancer remained it could spread, destroying my bladder and other organs too. I explained how I felt to Dr Syed in the hope that he could destroy the cancer while still leaving me with a bladder. Thankfully, private healthcare gives you a bit more flexibility with treatment in that way.

"Doctor, I understand what you're saying, but if any of the cancer remains and spreads, it might cost me my bladder anyway and my life too. If there's a chance that you can save both my bladder and my life, even if it's a slim one, please just take it. Shaving off as much of my bladder as I can live without might be the only way!"

"Very well then," said Dr Syed in his usual upliftingly determined voice. "We'll give it one more try but I can't make any guarantees."

"Thank you, Doctor!" I exclaimed so loudly and appreciatively that a few of his colleagues in nearby rooms probably heard too. "My whole family appreciates your efforts so much."

125

No Problem is Permanent

Dr Syed then sat back in his chair and smiled. "I know you do, Lloyd. If anyone can beat this again, you can."

Miraculously, the further surgery was a huge success. From the brink of disaster, I'd survived again. The cancer was decimated and I was left with a bladder. But to ensure that any presence of cancer lingering around in my body was completely obliterated, an even bigger challenge was still to come: yet more chemo. I had to accept that my life was about to be plunged into another extended difficult patch, when only a fortnight ago, life had felt like it couldn't get better. As well as the battles that every new business owner goes through, I now also had to fight both a disease that was trying to kill me and the memory of my last ordeal with cancer.

# Pulling through together...

The chemo was worse than I ever could have imagined. Without my *Fidelis* team and Naomi's continuing support, I probably wouldn't have made it through. They all knew how difficult this process would be for me, and so they all attended my first chemo session together. That meant so much. Instead of celebrating their growing list of accomplishments, the team was supporting and celebrating me.

Even though we hadn't quite grown a Happiness-Centred Business yet, we already had a happiness-centred team. Everything was in place for *Fidelis* to achieve incredible success on both human and corporate levels. In previous businesses, I'd felt as though it always fell to me to drive growth. Looking around my hospital room that day, I knew that the team could drive that growth, leaving me to focus my energies on beating cancer (again).

I still remember Sue Evans saying to me, "There's no way you're dying from this, Lloyd. It's just not happening; you are going to beat this! You'll pull through just like Prof Cruickshank said. Then we can all enjoy this growth together. We're changing the industry and a few tumours aren't going to get in our way."

She also helped me to process a profound and quite upsetting letter that I picked off the doormat after returning home from that session. The letter was from the Burton *NHS* team. It began:

"*Dear Mr Ansermoz,*

It's just what we do around here

*We have booked you an urgent appointment next Wednesday for surgery to remove your 3 grade 4 tumours. Please attend hospital by 11am this Saturday to prepare for this extensive surgery."*

The next part just seemed like a blur:

*"What to expect: XXXXXXXX"*

I didn't read that part as I almost dropped the letter in shock. If I'd waited that long for surgery, I would probably have died waiting for the appointment. Thinking about your death is a truly chilling, awful experience. The whole team rallied round me to help me process what I'd just read. After that, I gathered enough composure to call the team in Burton and cancel the appointment. Sometimes, despite the very best efforts of the hugely talented range of staff who have made the *NHS* what it is, they can only treat so many people at a time. There are often hundreds of people in queues for appointments and sometimes you've just got to wait. In those circumstances, particularly when you're facing an urgent health crisis which just can't wait, the more tailored treatment options offered by private healthcare can give you the lifeline you need. I will always be grateful, not just to my doctors, but also for the career that allowed me to purchase and retain private health insurance. While pushing for the appointment you need can often prove key in getting seen more quickly on the *NHS*, sometimes more quickly isn't quick enough.

Sue said, "Thank God for Dr Syed!" as soon as I showed her the letter. I couldn't have agreed more.

Sue was the most talented accountant, but more importantly was becoming one of the best friends I'd ever met, by a country mile. Sue had helped hugely in turning around the decline during *Keen Kleen*'s toughest years and building the business back into a structure which was stable enough for me to sell to Peter and *Indepth*. Laurence had introduced us after meeting her in the corporate world. Sue had worked as the finance director (FD) for what would become the home retail giant *Homebase*. Since then, she'd partnered with Laurence and was probably his most trusted adviser. He never let me down on business referrals and introductions. I will always be immensely grateful to them both for their contributions and proudly gave them equity stakes in *Fidelis*.

## No Problem is Permanent

Every business needs a Sue. After a first meeting with her following Laurence's introduction, our second meeting opened my eyes to a whole new level of corporate governance and financial planning. Previous meetings with the accountant I'd had for years went something along the lines of:

"You OK, Lloyd? Are you making a few quid? Yep, I can see that. Keep doing what you're doing and everything will be fine."

Sue, who had already had a quick browse through *Keen Kleen*'s numbers had a very different take.

"Lloyd, your business is insolvent!" are words that I'll never forget.

Only a few years back, we'd been buying businesses, and now Sue was telling me that *Keen Kleen*'s cash was about to run out completely. For the first time in quite a while, words failed me. There isn't really a textbook reaction for when someone tells you that your business is actually an office built on sand.

"How can that have happened??? We're a multi-million turnover business!" was my reaction after an awkwardly long pause.

"You *were*. There's no easy way of telling you this, Lloyd, but all that money has been spent. *Keen Kleen* has been spending tens of thousands of pounds every, single week. There's no way that even a long-established SME could cope with this level of expenditure."

The worrying truth was that I had no idea of the full extent of what had happened. With everything that had been going on in my personal life, I'd taken my eye off the ball. Sue was right. Turnover had dropped significantly (particularly after losing the deal with *Virgin*) but somehow, spending had increased. The wrong people had been making the wrong decisions around me. Worst of all, I'd been overly trusting and had waved through far too many things without giving specific matters the careful attention that they deserved. While no problem is permanent, no single success lasts forever either. If you don't keep working on yourself and constantly trying to improve, then you'll struggle to sustain that success and manifest it into better long-term futures for both yourself and your team. It was obvious that the only thing for me to do was to give Sue immediate control over all of our accounts on the best terms we could agree.

Sue then introduced me to the wonderful Gill who came in 3-4 days a week to sort our bookkeeping out. Things slowly got back on an even keel and *Keen Kleen* eventually started to get back to

## It's just what we do around here

£34k monthly net profit and kept going from there. Sadly, problems that preceded both Sue and Gill continued to engulf the business and they advised that the best way forwards was to liquidate the company and move on after ensuring we fully paid off our debts to clear the decks for a new start under the same brand. The only way for the company to survive those immediate challenges was in a new structure. Peter eventually acquired the business in its new structure further down the line.

Years later, I remained hugely grateful for Sue's wisdom and support. She was one of the first people I called after leaving *Indepth* and without her tireless work, there's no way that we would have even got *Fidelis* off the ground, let alone successfully sold the business in 2021.

After promising Peter that any new business I started wouldn't approach any of his clients, the entire *Fidelis* team had their work cut-out to persuade our first few partners that we could offer them world-class service. Sue made sure that all the pressure I'd felt in those final few years at *Keen Kleen* before the liquidation wasn't a part of our new venture. Everyone could talk to her about almost anything. She was an immensely gifted listener and always kept the confidence of anyone she spoke to. Knowing that I would absolutely throw myself back into work after my surgery (and probably end up more ill as a result), Sue encouraged me to make the journey back to my full schedule gradually.

She'd often say, "Just focus on doing something positive each day first. Try to do something to push the business forwards and don't worry too much about the hours you're working. I'll handle all the accounts to make sure we pay regular bills and invoices, and email all the documents to you, so you won't have to worry about keeping the business on an even keel. I'll regularly brief you on everything too so that you'll never need to worry about being out of the loop. You can just put all your energy into meeting partners and building lasting partnerships. The last thing you need is to come home to hours of admin after all that. The prospect of doing anything now will feel like an uphill struggle, but you will beat this and things will get easier. Then when you're back at full speed, everything will be running smoothly. You'll slot right back into your usual role."

Having never been one of those colleagues who made promises without actioning positive improvements, Sue also helped me to feel as normal as possible in a couple of my chemo sessions by holding finance and budget planning discussions in the middle of them.

There was no, "Oh, are you sure you can manage with this, Lloyd?" or "Should I come back tomorrow?"

Sue just got straight into the nitty gritty and acted as if we were in a board room and I wasn't attached to a drip. It was almost an inconvenience when nurses occasionally interrupted our meetings. I could see her politely holding back from sighing loudly while a nurse adjusted a bag of fluid during a quarterly P&L forecast. This helped me hugely as for the length of that meeting, the cancer felt like it wasn't there anymore. We were having a business meeting in a slightly different location to normal, but it was the same meeting as usual. Everybody has their own way of coping with chemo. For me, pushing it to the side and focusing on work was essential to growing through the adversity attacking my bladder and looking towards a brighter future.

# Great things come from getting little things right...

One of the best meetings we had was when Sue came into my room at the hospital celebrating some amazing news. "Lloyd, we've just won a very interesting new contract! Our partner will be a retirement village in Birmingham with big plans. Do you remember the company that Carl [one of the best people we ever hired] was working for before he joined us? It's them!" I remembered them very well and was over the moon.

The £35,000 contract agreed with the retirement village was one of the smaller ones that *Fidelis* signed at that time, thanks to some wonderful prior support from Birmingham's industrial community. Some of our competitors at the time might have dismissed this deal as Only a 'little' job. We didn't.

While we were trying to create a new era of managed services, the retirement village was changing their own sector forever. They were (and still remain) committed not just to affordable living in retirement, but also to providing residents with an enormous range of activities and facilities. Everything from music to chess and sports were on offer in the first villages they built. Bigger villages with their own shopping centres would follow. But before those developments took shape, the *Fidelis* team had to ensure that our

It's just what we do around here

newest partner's village in Aston was pristine and made residents who had moved from homes with carefully tended back gardens feel like they were still right at home. Few experiences are more personal than popping to the loo and you'll never feel at home anywhere with grubby and unpleasant washrooms. That's why our first job with this wonderful company involved looking after their washrooms and kitting them out with brand-new kit. The latest versions of scrubber-dryers and other essentials appeared across the Aston Cross village, giving residents and staff experiences they loved. A few months into this deal my phone rang again. Sue had been right. What had started as a small but very exciting partnership was about to become one of the relationships on which *Fidelis* anchored its growth.

Sally, who furnished our newest partner's retirement villages phoned and said:

"Your team has made quite an impression, Lloyd. Head Office is delighted and our Directors would like to sit down with you as soon as possible. We are seeking planning permission for a new village on the Hagley Road, near Edgbaston. As you know, this is one of Birmingham's most prestigious postcodes and residents will expect us to go above and beyond if they are going to move into one of these new homes. The new village will have its own bar, grocer, hairdresser and barber as part of a luxury new shopping centre. We're building up to 400 new homes here and we need your advice on how to maintain the whole thing. We just don't trust any other provider with a project of this magnitude.

When can you meet?"

Receiving an enquiry like this was a huge compliment to everyone who had given their all to help this unique leader in supported living to achieve their goals. In business you never know where your next project might come from, so treating each one like your last is absolutely essential. Great things will develop from there.

I had to pause celebrating this exciting new development and reply to Sally's very kind offer:

"Thank you so much for calling, Sally, it's a real joy to hear about how the *Fidelis* team is helping your new residents to ease into this exciting new phase of their lives. It would be a pleasure to meet next week and discuss how we can expand our wonderful partnership."

Things only got better during the meeting that followed in Coventry. *Fidelis* were retained as consultants overseeing the

## No Problem is Permanent

entire project, on an improved contract of £100,000 a year. This was a staggering achievement for a business that was still technically a startup. Sally's CEO didn't have any doubts in awarding us the contract though.

I remember him saying, "Lloyd, people are recommending our homes to their parents and grandparents. If we get this wrong, families' lives might be challenged permanently. That cannot happen. We need you because you truly understand the little things. Some managed services providers might leave marks on mirrors. There might be a towel in the wrong place next to the sink or some paper next to the bin. They think that's OK. Your team would never settle for leaving a washroom looking just OK. You always do the whole job to the highest standard, all of the time. We want that in every room, business, office, washroom, dining area and communal space in our villages. We want people to trust us to care for their loved ones as they would. Our residents need to feel at home every day. That all only happens if we trust you to keep doing what you're doing across everything, every day. I'm confident that you'll deliver on this and that we can trust *Fidelis* with even more large projects like this in future."

His kind words only reinforced my view that the things that people often say "nobody will notice" constantly get noticed. The more shortcuts any organisation takes in their presentation, then the more doubts potential partners will have about working with them. For example, imagine you walk into a co-working building and meet with the manager to discuss the possibility of renting one of their larger office spaces. They make you a hot drink as you walk in and everything is going well - until you lift your mug and look at the coaster underneath. It's got tea stains on it (and not small ones either). That just completely puts you off and makes you doubt the business so much. What else isn't right? What other things did they think you wouldn't see... or you would see but just not care about?

Another of Dr Paddi Lund's wonderful books, *The Absolutely Critical Non-Essentials,* talks about those little things which aren't essential for your business to operate but make all the difference in how your partners perceive the quality of service they're receiving. These critical non-essentials cover not just coasters but also fresh flowers, selections of refreshments, tea and coffee service and personalised greetings. After all, it's always nice if the front desk knows who you are when you walk in, not just when they're sending you an invoice. Re-investing in your

It's just what we do around here

business isn't just about boosting sales. It's about showing your gratitude to your partners for their support and placing their happiness next to the happiness of your colleagues - right at the heart of your business.

At our *Fidelis* offices, we served our partners tea and coffee in beautiful cups and saucers that cost a fortune. They chose their preferred beverages from our drinks menu, including fine wine and cold drinks. We were literally investing thousands of pounds every year in quality and welcoming refreshments for our partners and colleagues. Some people thought that this was a waste of money and wondered if I'd lost my mind, particularly after *Keen Kleen*'s financial challenges. As with everything though, Sue understood exactly why this expenditure mattered so much and was delighted to authorise it. If you're in someone's office discussing a potential partnership worth £500,000 over five years, you don't expect to drink cold tea from chipped mugs that seemed like a great purchase a few Christmases ago. The whole experience must feel like the millions of pounds worth of value that you'd receive over the course of the partnership. Sue was absolutely determined to sign off any expenditure which would make anybody setting foot into an increasingly growing *Fidelis* office feel like they were getting VIP treatment that very few other managed services providers even considered offering them.

A 'do em if you can' mentality was the norm in every aspect of the industry at the time. That applied to jobs themselves as well as the quality of the experiences that providers created in their offices for any partners or potential partners who visited. Missing a spot was often seen as standard and many providers hoped that 'clients' (who they never saw as partners) would tolerate and then pay for jobs that were never quite done after discussing deals in meeting rooms that were never quite pristine. Our *Fidelis* team believed in doing all of the work that we were paid to do to the highest possible standards and in using our spaces as case studies for the results that our partners received as standard procedure. Nothing would 'just do' and so our team vigorously applied the idea of critical non-essentials to cover the jobs that others just couldn't be bothered to do across absolutely everything we did.

I personally became an expert in not just flowers and the symmetry of orchids, but in evaluating the spaces that we maintained in the minutest of detail. I'd always had an eye for detail, but this was different gravy. All of my colleagues embraced that meticulous mentality too. This team focus ensured that every

## No Problem is Permanent

space associated with the *Fidelis* brand was always fresh and fragrant. Our partners absolutely loved the care that our operatives (both on site and in the *Fidelis* office) took in and around their spaces. They also noticed and appreciated the time spent on creating a pleasant, calming and welcoming environment for us to share their company in, whenever they popped into our Head Office.

Having spent more than enough time in GPs' surgeries before setting up *Fidelis*, I also decided that there was absolutely no way those uncomfortable chairs were coming anywhere near our office. The team agreed. Beautiful, luxurious furniture in warm colours then filled our foyer, meeting rooms and individual offices.

In the same meeting where Sue told me about that first opportunity to work with a national leader in supported living, we then spent 20 minutes talking about the chair that our wonderful receptionist sat in every day. It's difficult to relax other people if you've got to spend all day sitting in a chair that conforms to *Health and Safety Executive (HSE)* standards but still leaves you feeling uncomfortable. Other businesses might have dismissed anything beyond the bare minimum of interest in receptionists' chairs as pointless. *Fidelis* thought differently. We bought a specialist ergonomically designed chair to keep both sides of our front desk experience as comfy as possible.

The same thinking was behind *Fidelis* paying our operatives' travel expenses. Turning up to work looking focused, relaxed and ready to deliver world-class service becomes a nightmare if you're walking through the pouring rain and panicking, after missing the bus to save money. Part of world-class service involves impeccable punctuality, and so the business made sure that our operatives always had the resources to get wherever they needed to be, early.

One of our competitors once asked Carl how *Fidelis* were able to do all of this. Carl replied with seven of the best words I've ever heard:

"It's just what we do around here!"

It's just what we do around here

# Your network is bigger than you think...

Carl was the first person *Fidelis* employed full-time. He would become one of our highest trained people and exemplified the company's values. Every business needs those colleagues who just get things done without ever compromising on quality and never showing the company in a bad light. Carl was never interested in office politics or drama. His only focus was on inspiring others by doing the best work he possibly could every day, no matter how he was feeling. The many commendations he would receive as *Fidelis* grew came from there. Without his phenomenal work ethic and deep understanding and appreciation of our company's values, some of our most important partnerships would have collapsed. Without Carl, we never would have even been in touch with the supported living pioneer.

Sadly, some business owners don't create the best possible environments for people like Carl to thrive because they don't invest enough in their people. If you're asking yourself whether to give your people bonuses at Christmas, Easter or other important public holidays, stop asking and just do it. If brilliant people feel underappreciated, they'll leave. The cost of losing them is then almost always more expensive than the cost of keeping them.

As usual, the deal that enabled *Fidelis* to hire Carl full-time came from a phone call.

"Our current provider is an absolute nightmare! Genuinely terrible! I don't know what to do..." sighed Lisa Ausden down the other end of the line.

Lisa worked for *IAC*, who produced luxurious and decadent carpets into high-end sports cars. After touring their main sight in Coleshill, it became clear that I had much more in common with Lisa than an interest in pristine factories. Her son Simon was in a long-term relationship with my niece, Mel. We sealed the £47,000 that got *Fidelis* off the ground only a few months after setting up and the partnership with *IAC* only grew from there. They were the first business to trust us to service them: our first partners. Lisa would introduce me to her colleague, Julie, whose Bickenhill site faced multiple maintenance challenges. Carl happened to be one of the operatives already working there who was committed to turning things around. This new £75,000 a year contract gave

No Problem is Permanent

*Fidelis* the resources that we needed to employ Carl and colleagues who shared his view of things.

This chain of events only emphasised how much your own personal network matters when setting up a business. Almost everyone will know someone who might need your services. Many people think of personal networks as the rich people talking to their rich friends, but in truth, everyone has a network. Let's say your friend runs a florist's. Why would you buy your flowers online from a big corporation instead of going straight to your friend? If some of your other friends switch to your friend's new business too and then you all leave great reviews on *Google*, your florist mate will be off to a cracking start.

Lisa had no idea that I was Mel's uncle before she picked up the phone to me. That just shows how many people around you don't actually realise how much they can support you before you get chatting to them about your business. I never thought to ring Lisa either. When you set up a business, phone your friends, family, distant cousins and anyone else you know to tell them all about your new venture. You never know who could help you and how. Sadly, I still had fences to mend with some of my relatives after leaving the family business all those years earlier. That significantly limited who I could reach out to when we set up *Fidelis*. If (happily) you don't find yourself in that position, pick-up the phone (or drop people a message) and don't miss out on support that's sitting right in front of you. You might be surprised at just how many of your family and friends will be delighted to help you.

When you get that first sale as a new business, you need proper people processes in place to support a promising and committed team as they develop their skills and turn one sale into many. Their professional development builds shared values and attitudes into a team journey towards a thriving company. Carl, Sue, Gill and the team all played essential roles in supporting that development, but perhaps the biggest role of all in *Fidelis'* story, my business career and my life in general was played by Laurence. Before joining our team, Laurence had built a hugely successful career in helping executives of household-name brands like *John Lewis* to make their next moves. When we first met, I was expecting him to wish me all the best but, unfortunately, be too busy to work with me.

The reality couldn't have been further from that. Laurence not only played a crucial role in preparing *Keen Kleen* for its eventual sale but also ensured that *Fidelis* had all the people processes that you'd expect to find in a multi-million pound turnover business before we'd even started.

# Brilliant people make businesses profitable...

When I first spoke to him about the idea that became *Fidelis*, Laurence said, "Lloyd, you've got to run this new business like the multi-million pound business you want it to become. Otherwise, you're unlikely to achieve the selling price forecast in your plan. Investors and buyers love certainty and they will only buy *Fidelis* for your forecast price if they have absolute confidence in your people. You'll give them all the confidence they need that they're inheriting a top team from you by giving your outstanding people equally outstanding training. This training will provide your people with a clear internal roadmap of how to deliver a culture of world class care and customer service while working smoothly with you and your leadership team. Gaps in coaching and leadership in your team will blow holes in that confidence and put a successful future sale of *Fidelis* at enormous risk."

We started as we meant to go on. Under Laurence's invaluable input and guidance, this new and ambitious startup adopted the same practices and protocols during Board meetings as some of the most famous companies in the UK. Meetings were organised through a timed agenda which everyone respected, and meticulously minuted. Attendance, which was required from our leadership team, was always exemplary anyway because the whole team shared the same drive to succeed. Individual performance reports were required to be submitted a week before meetings and always following the 14$^{th}$ of the month. This allowed for informed strategic decision-making while allowing our accountancy team ample time to deliver monthly finance reports to the highest degree of accuracy. Discussions were thorough, fair and balanced. Most importantly, nobody left a *Fidelis* Board meeting feeling as though they hadn't been heard.

Sadly though, these processes didn't stop our Board getting a particularly nasty surprise during a meeting that I'll remember forever for all the wrong reasons. A colleague who had journeyed with me through several different firms hadn't been themselves

## No Problem is Permanent

lately. They hadn't been looking after themselves as well as they used to. Their timekeeping had also slipped noticeably. I won't name them here as I still respect them for all they did and regret that events had to unfold as they did.

This trusted colleague attended a Board meeting and immediately raised more than a few eyebrows. They arrived drunk at 10 am. It was impossible not to notice as they almost fell asleep on the table mid-meeting. I had to ask them to leave the room. Then came the question of what to do next. I was conflicted given my long-term personal and professional relationship with the individual, but Laurence was clear.

"Lloyd," he said ruefully but unhesitatingly, "We can't have that in this room or anywhere in the business. I know you want to help this person but that sentiment can't obstruct the growth we're trying to build. I appreciate that this is hugely difficult for you, but my advice would be to let them go, today if possible."

It wasn't just Laurence making these observations. Other Board members had expressed concerns about this colleague's performance for weeks. That meeting had been the final straw.

I took their counsel and advice seriously and the conversation I'd been dreading for a while followed. I told our colleague that as a board we had lost confidence in their abilities, and they no longer had a place at *Fidelis*. Sadly, they haven't spoken to me since.

Life as a leader and business owner involves putting the long-term success of the company ahead of anything that you might be feeling personally. That can often result in a series of immensely tough decisions. Although they might hurt you at the time, you'll look back down the road and realise that you made the right choices.

One of the most enjoyable aspects of business ownership for me was helping people to build meaningful careers for themselves that transformed both their own lives and those of their families. That was why letting anybody go was never a decision that I enjoyed making. However, as sad as that particular incident was for me personally, nothing and nobody was going to stop *Fidelis* from growing to its full potential. The business moved on and immensely special and talented people continued to join our team.

Paula started working as a cleaning operative a few hours for us every week between school runs. She remained committed and rose to become one of our senior operations managers within a four-year period. It has been an absolute pleasure to watch her continuing and relentless career growth. I still remember my first

It's just what we do around here

conversation with Paula. She popped into the office first thing one morning, just as I was getting in.

A slightly nervous person standing opposite me interrupted my phone scrolling after I'd had a quick chat with our wonderful receptionist.

"Hello, can I help you?" I asked, wanting to be as helpful to our unexpected new friend as possible. After all, unexpected new friends didn't arrive every day, so it seemed like this person was offering something very special. As it happened, Paula was.

"Hello, my name's Paula. I hope you don't mind me turning up, but can I drop my CV into reception?" she answered with her usual charm and impeccable manners.

"I haven't worked in a while because I've been looking after my kids, but I've got loads of skills and am looking for a few hours work in between picking them up from school. I promise you - you won't be let down!"

It's not every day that you get approached by people asking for an opportunity. Most people just fill out forms and wait to hear back. It takes something special to have the initiative to apply in-person like that and have the willingness to prove yourself.

"Great to meet you Paula, I'm Lloyd, one of the Directors here. If you give your CV to me, I'll drop it into reception for you. I'm sure we'll have something. Is it OK if we have a read through and one of my colleagues, Ian, gives you a call back today?"

Paula's face lit up and we shook hands. I was determined that she'd get a call back for better or worse, as it's never nice to leave people hanging - especially when you receive quality and confident job applications.

"Wow!" was the first thing that Laurence said when I phoned him to chew over what had happened. "So long as Ian is happy with her joining the team, why don't you give her a few hours and see if she turns up? Then if she does a good job, we can give her some more."

That seemed fair and so Paula got her first shift as a cleaning operative with *Fidelis*. We never looked back. She was an inspiration and did some of the most impressive work we'd seen in some time. Her fantastic career and rapid rise to leadership in the coming years was no surprise at all. Paula's growth as a leader was testament to both her exemplary professional attitude and her unwavering drive to join us on our journey to create a great business. More importantly, however, this growth was exactly

139

## No Problem is Permanent

what her utter determination to create a great life for herself and her family deserved.

Ryan's career with us followed a similar pattern. I recently saw him driving around town in the awesome company car he's earned in a new leadership role elsewhere and couldn't have been prouder.

Paula, Ryan and many others knew that they could build prosperous careers in managed services because I had. As a leader you can't ask someone to do something that you haven't done yourself. Not many executives have had the experience of cleaning a toilet after a work Christmas party. I've done that many times. My own experiences gave ambitious operatives at *Fidelis* a clear path to follow to enjoy the senior leadership careers that they knew they deserved, along with all of the perks that come within those roles.

Laurence was always there, playing an integral role in sustaining *Fidelis'* growth from employing a few wonderful people to almost 500. Like Sue, he earned equity in our business on a ratchet basis. As the business grew, their stakes grew too.

Laurence also helped me with the most personal hire that *Fidelis* ever made. My son, Ian, was showing huge promise in supervision and leadership roles elsewhere and wanted to join the business. I knew that he could make a massively positive impact, but also wanted to avoid any impression that I was giving my son a fast-track over other colleagues. Laurence helped me to fit Ian into our operations team perfectly, and, to Ian's immense credit, he impressed everyone. Ian eventually began leading on some of our key projects and went on to lead the entire operation of the business. After continuing to lead *Fidelis* post-sale, Ian was keen to launch his own business as soon as he could. He is now running his own very successful business in managed services thanks to his unique approach to values, culture and customer service. I am immensely proud of the businessman and leader he has become.

Probably one of the most important project Ian led before *Fidelis* was sold involved managing our relationship with the *NHS*. The overwhelming majority of the housekeeping teams throughout *NHS* Trusts do wonderful work every day and receive generous benefits packages that reflect their tireless and painstaking work. However, a small minority were taking significant time off all at the same time, leaving a leading Trust short-staffed for an extended period. These talented professionals

It's just what we do around here

had earned these periods of rest and there was nothing that the Trust could do to bring them back to work more quickly.

The Trust turned to *Fidelis* to help relieve pressure on rotas that was beginning to impact the quality of the care they offered. Our operational team worked closely within the *Care Quality Commission's* guidelines and the national *NHS* requirements for managing cleanliness to the highest standards.

We set out to train more than 50 people to deliver the highest possible standards of cleaning throughout the Trust's hospitals, wards and theatres. On one occasion, we facilitated the operation of a key hospital's entire housekeeping team on one shift to ensure that its various departments operated smoothly. That afternoon, a major surgical procedure had significantly run over into the night and the hospital's housekeeping team had gone home after a busy day. Without our support, nobody would have been available to clean the area where the surgery had taken place that night. The hospital team would then have had no choice but to close the entire area the next morning, cancelling multiple surgeries in the process.

Thanks to our people's efforts, this crucial space was cleaned thoroughly after the late-running surgery. The following day's surgeries then went ahead as planned. The Trust therefore gladly paid us increased rates per operative, per hour, matching the pay rates earnt by their highly trained and skilled housekeeping team members. They called us whenever one of their team members was unavailable and they needed a trained and fully authorised individual from our bank of talented operatives to cover for them. This was above our average rates by a further 25%. Obviously, we paid our own highly trained and skilled teams 25% above the average pay rates at that time too.

A long-term friendship and valued relationship with Delia Cannings proved invaluable from the start. Delia is the most trusted professional training lead in the cleaning industry across the country and specialises in healthcare environments. Delia and her team at her fantastic business, *Environmental Excellence,* were pivotal to the success of our highly trained teams. On this project, *Environmental Excellence* pulled out all the stops by taking every member of those teams to the highest *NHS* approved standards as qualified and certified professionals in a matter of just a few weeks.

Ian was integral to the success of this relationship and to building the relationship with the *CQC* that underpinned it. The

## No Problem is Permanent

*CQC* would go on to consult us when preparing their official guidance for Trusts on how hospitals, wards and theatres should be maintained.

I remember giving him a copy of their official guidance document after it was published. "Ian, I'm so proud of you!" was the only thing I could say. After my own relationship with my Dad, I was determined to celebrate Ian and his successes when the two of us were chatting, not just when I was chatting to my friends.

As Ian took on more and more responsibility within *Fidelis*, Sally called me again. Our work with the rapidly expanding family of retirement villages now spanned sites stretching to High Wycombe and beyond. They weren't even putting contracts out to tender anymore. They just came straight to us. The relationship that had been built over multiple years since the initial £35,000 contract to a value of £700,000 annually.

Sally had more good news.

"Lloyd, it would be much easier for us to go to one single provider for both our Hard and Soft FM services. We know you've done such an outstanding job with the Soft side, so we wanted to ask whether you could save us a headache and cover our Hard FM services too?"

Despite the effort that the whole *Fidelis* team had gone to in making the term 'managed services' a thing, Hard and Soft FM had been staples of industry lexicon for so long that partners often just referred to them instinctively. Only a few years ago, we had been the new kids on the block, and it takes generations to change an entire industry's habits.

My immediate response to Sally was, "Thanks so much for your continuing trust in *Fidelis*. We can certainly help you with that. Can I put you in touch with my colleague, Ian, and he'll get back to you with some proposals as soon as possible?"

An elated "That would be wonderful thanks, Lloyd. I look forward to meeting Ian in the very near future!" came back down the line.

It was the best response I could have hoped for and gave us the time we needed to add premium level maintenance of lifts, lighting, heating, plumbing and all those other things that make buildings tick to our managed services offering.

Ian led on finding an elite provider who could partner with us to provide these services to the world-class standards that the retirement village conglomerate's team expected. After

It's just what we do around here

interviewing dozens of providers, he felt like he'd found the perfect partner. The whole team agreed and a £5 million deal was in sight. This would be the biggest deal we'd ever done and would push *Fidelis* into a completely different stratosphere.

Then disaster struck.

The provider we'd planned to partner with collapsed suddenly without any warning. One day a business can be on top of the world, and then the next, its owners can be pulling the shutters down. If ever we needed a reminder to remain grateful for every day we were in business (even the nightmare ones), that was it. I still vividly remember the phone call in which we found out how bad the situation was. Ian had spoken to the company privately earlier that day and organised a conference call between their Board and ours shortly afterwards.

Their CEO, Greg, delivered the bad news.

"I'm so, so sorry. Due to major cash flow difficulties, our business has no option but to close. This is absolutely devastating for all of us personally and professionally as our entire staff will now lose their jobs. As a result, this obviously means that we'll have to withdraw from our proposed partnership with your team. Letting you down like that really hurts. This is a career low for me personally as CEO and I stepped down this morning without seeking any further personal compensation."

"Greg," I said, "Closing down is probably the worst part of business life. It happens to the best of us and you've got absolutely nothing to be ashamed of. Please let your team and operatives know that we'd be more than happy to give their CVs a good look."

The Board shared my sentiments and the call ended amicably. We were all hugely grateful to Ian for including us all on the call, as it gave us an opportunity to focus on helping Greg rather than sharing a few frustrated and disappointed email chains regretting the lost deal.

Sally showed us nothing but kindness, empathy and understanding when Ian told her what had happened.

"Thank you so much for going to all that effort to help us. While we'll now need to look elsewhere for a Hard FM services provider, this also means that a separate nationwide Soft FM contract will go out to tender shortly. While we'd normally come straight to you, we're required to put this out to tender due to the scope of the opportunity. We'd hugely appreciate it if you could submit a bid though. As your team has looked after some of our most important sites so well for so long, I'm sure that you could enter a very competitive bid."

Ian had a bid prepared within weeks and *Fidelis* were awarded the tender after a hugely competitive process involving 4 other businesses. This separate nationwide contract was worth £1.2 million a year for 5 years. It's not every day that terrible news can lead to you landing more than five million pounds in new business. It didn't happen to *Fidelis* because of luck. Luck is what businesses that don't have exceptional teams rely on. Exceptional teams rely on their faith in each other and shared loyalty to achieve outstanding results.

Having such faith in everyone on your team may seem like a strange (or even intimidating) concept, but at *Fidelis*, this was just what we did.

As our business grew, many investors increased their faith in us, but we didn't take on any external investment for 9 years from 2011-2020. As 2021 approached, it became clear that a number of investors were looking to buy *Fidelis* in its entirety. The question now was not just about whether potential buyers could offer the level of finance required to buy the business, but whether they shared our values too.

A specialist M&A company offered to help us find a buyer who could do both. That was how I met Tony Vaughan.

# Chapter Eleven

## Full circle

"Lloyd, don't risk your life's work. Make sure that you scrutinise potential buyers of *Fidelis* for cultural compatibility. If they don't share your values, then they won't nurture the seeds that you've planted to keep the business growing. Finding a buyer who aligns with everything you stand for is the only way to ensure that *Fidelis* continues as an industry leader for the next 10 years."

That was Tony's pitch. Every other broker attempting to sell *Fidelis* only ever talked about money. Tony genuinely cared about our company culture and preserving the core values that sat at the heart of the £multi-million annual turnover that our business was now generating.

Shortly before we'd set up *Fidelis* in 2011, Tony set up *Vexus Corporate*, which helps entrepreneurs to sell their businesses on ideal terms. Having built and sold hugely successful businesses over several decades, Tony saw *a lot* about the process of business sales that he wanted to improve. *Vexus* came from there. He wanted to solve the same problems in his sector that I'd wanted to solve in mine. Tony felt that too many brokers only focused on commission and did not appreciate just how much business sales change founders' lives. He also understood that clients are partners who need tailored solutions. If *Fidelis* had one founding idea - that was it. Tony was (and remains) committed to making a real difference to people's lives through his work. That same commitment had powered me through both the happiest and the darkest days of *Fidelis*. The amount we shared in common was staggering.

## Never sell your business through or to just anyone…

Tony did something else that really stood out to me. He actually bothered to get to know me and the *Fidelis* team. Everyone else just sent endless emails telling me how high a final sale price they could secure and always forgot to ask one very simple question - what did the *Fidelis* shareholders want both for ourselves and for the future of the business? The other brokers spamming us weren't interested in anything apart from signing *Fidelis* up as a client. Tony had none of that about him. He focused solely on helping us deliver our own goals rather than trying to choose our goals for us.

A few of his first questions to me were:

"What motivated you to start *Fidelis*? What kind of future do you see for the business? How would you like your team to be looked after in any sales process?"

The first response that came to mind was, "Well, we definitely want anyone in the existing team to be treated in exactly the same way by new ownership as we treat them. Our operatives deserve both certainty about their work and opportunities to continue thriving in fulfilling careers. None of our current shareholders would ever want to profit at the expense of our operatives' futures.

"It's also crucial that whoever buys *Fidelis* truly understands the difference between our approach to partnership and the perception of clients as 'contracts' that has held the industry back for so long. Business ownership means far more than just making

## Full circle

money to me and the rest of the team. Making a permanent positive difference to the industry and the millions of people who depend on it to earn their living, work in safe spaces or build their business across the UK, matters more to us than anything else."

After hearing something like that, most sales people ignore most of what you've said, and just try to spin you a load of spiel based very loosely on a few of the ideas you mentioned - not Tony.

"I was hoping you'd say that and couldn't agree with you more!" was his almost perfect reply.

"The whole point of building a business is to improve people's lives. One of the main reasons I started *Vexus* was to ensure that both entrepreneurs and the businesses they launch can grow through ownership changes. A business sale doesn't just involve cash meeting bank accounts and stocks meeting portfolios. The process requires a meeting of minds too. Aligning a potential buyer's aims and sector expertise with existing company growth objectives reassures entrepreneurs that their businesses will stay in safe hands under new ownership. Financial negotiations can then flow from those assurances."

Then something else extraordinary happened.

Tony and I started speaking regularly for hours about our experiences of business ownership. It's very rare that you get a chance to spend time with other entrepreneurs and just chat about life. So much of every day is spent thinking about your next email, call or project that you rarely get time just to talk about your experiences with someone who's been through the same situations as you. Whilst support from your loved ones is invaluable for any entrepreneur, you can learn so much from reflecting on business life with people who've encountered similar challenges to you when running their own companies.

Tony didn't need to sell *Fidelis*. *Vexus* already had dozens of sales under its belt and was thriving commercially. Tony wanted to sell *Fidelis* because I was his sort of entrepreneur. Likewise, he stood for everything that I stood for. That's why he stood apart from everyone else pitching to me at the time.

After I'd gotten to know Tony, I introduced him to the team and it was a match made in heaven.

Once he'd visited the office, Sue said to me, "He's got to be the one who sells our business, hasn't he? None of the other brokers even come close."

## No Problem is Permanent

Ian and Laurence agreed, and we signed with *Vexus*. Then the work of finding the perfect buyer for *Fidelis* began.

Whilst our business had achieved a lot in some areas, we didn't take on projects in others. One of the areas in which we took on less work was reactive cleaning, which occurs when you're called out in an emergency (usually to an industrial site setting) to clean affected areas and make them safe. The perfect sale would be one that our buyers would perceive as an accretive acquisition - where *Fidelis* added services to their offering and they offered services to ours. Tony played an absolute blinder and discovered that the Derbyshire-based *REACT Group plc* were looking to make exactly that type of purchase. They had made a big impression both regionally and nationally with their emergency cleaning services. From industrial accidents to gut-wrenching traffic incidents and crime scenes, *REACT* were able to provide cleaning and decontamination services in places where other providers couldn't go. Everyone in the industry knew and respected their deep expertise in reactive cleaning and so when Tony mentioned their interest in *Fidelis*, having a conversation seemed like an obvious next step.

This time, the phone didn't ring. Tony organised a meeting between the *Fidelis* and *REACT* Boards to explore the possibility of moving forwards together as a larger and more agile company. Tony hosted us all in a neutral venue. *REACT*'s Chairman, Mark Braund, their CEO, and later their then CFO, couldn't have been more positive, helpful and inspiring at the time.

Whilst the exact exchanges can't be shared, they answered all of our questions and, most importantly, laid out exactly why acquiring *Fidelis* would add so much value to their business. The absolute last thing I wanted to do was to sell the business that we'd spent more than a decade building to a private equity firm who would just sack all of our talented operatives and sell the business on for a profit. Any sale of *Fidelis* needed to add to what we'd already built, keep as much of that as possible in place, and grow from there. Thankfully, that was exactly what *REACT* wanted to do. They loved not just the culture we'd built, but the results it was delivering. 87% of our work at the time was recurring, and no one partner represented more than 8% of our revenue. More importantly, even if *Fidelis* had lost our 10 most lucrative partnerships, we'd have still kept 50% of business revenue. Very few businesses can celebrate statistics like that. Those numbers

Full circle

were a testament not just to how many partners trusted us, but how long they had held that trust in us for.

Rather than changing what worked, *REACT* wanted to help *Fidelis* to make as big an impact in reactive cleaning services as we had in managed contract services. Mark was completely open with us all in saying that he'd had his eye on our list of Education and Healthcare partners for some time and would love to offer them reactive cleaning services. Earning trust in these sectors is hugely difficult and so providers of a whole range of services prize long-term relationships with the brands leading them. Buying the partnerships that we'd built was (almost) a priceless opportunity.

From a first meeting that couldn't have gone any better, our two businesses kept talking and then became one. On 29th March 2021, almost ten years to the day after *Fidelis* was incorporated as a company, *The Financial Times* carried the announcement that *REACT Group plc* had acquired our business in a £multi-million deal.

Possibly the only person happier about this announcement than me was Mark.

He told me, "This is not one of those deals where we're hoping to make money years down the line. Bringing your team into ours will start boosting our bottom line right now. Everyone is going to do very well from this. More importantly, we'll create a larger business which can help far more talented professionals to build wonderful careers in this sector. We both know that working in managed services transforms lives. Now the whole world is about to see just how much good we can create together."

A difficulty of selling any business is that things will never quite remain as you left them. There will be parts of the culture your team implemented that you wish were still in place. Post-sale, you'll often find yourself thinking, "What if the new owners still did *x*...?"

But that's another story for another day.

# Always be grateful for great people...

This wasn't one of those successes I'd experienced previously that tended to come weeks or months before some awful news. This

## No Problem is Permanent

was the wonderful conclusion of a decade's tireless work and meticulous planning from the whole *Fidelis* team. It's very rare that absolutely everything in a business plan you wrote so long ago plays out in front of you. That only happened because of the outstanding people I had around me and the talented community that we built together. It's important to be grateful when the right people come into your life. I'm still grateful to everyone who ever came through the doors of the *Fidelis* office. Particular thanks go to Sue and Laurence, who fully supported the project before we even had an office with doors. But my gratitude doesn't stop there. It extends to the Facilities Manager of the leading engineering company who took the time to listen to me before putting their complaint about "Stealing food" to one side and then valuing our operatives properly both as professionals and people.

Some of the best moments of owning any business happen when you leave a room knowing that the people you met will now look at a challenge or situation completely differently. If you can create value that changes outlooks and improves lives, success will come from there.

One of the most important factors in all the success we achieved was Naomi. If she hadn't seen what I couldn't see in the darkest moments of the years leading up to 2011, I might never have founded *Fidelis* in the first place. Without this wonderful business, hundreds of people would never have had the opportunity to demonstrate their talents; partners would have had to settle for less; and the company's founding team would never have earned life-changing rewards.

Looking back, it seems impossible to imagine my life missing the *Fidelis* chapter, but when I was recovering from Professor Cruickshank's surgery, nothing was certain. I had to regain the self-belief that had powered me through so many years in the industry and remember that behind the cancer, Lloyd the successful entrepreneur was still there. Alongside my renewed faith, Naomi's endless love and support made that possible.

When she told me all those years ago that building something even bigger and better than *Keen Kleen* was possible, I wasn't sure what to think.

My instant response was, "Do you really think I can do all that again on an even bigger scale? Battling this brain tumour has taken almost everything out of me. The thought of dealing with this exhausting recovery and the hassle of the last few years of *Keen Kleen* and employing even more people feels like too much."

Full circle

Then, Naomi freed me of all that doubt.

"If you have the right people around you, then nothing's too much. Laurence and Sue are amazing at what they do, Ian is ready to move forwards in his career, and there are dozens of people in the industry who would love to work with you again. Imagine if *Keen Kleen* had never gone through that difficult patch and you hadn't had to deal with all the personal drama that was happening in the background. The business would still be growing today. With proper people in place alongside a culture of care and better processes, I know that your new business will change hundreds of lives for years to come. Lloyd, there's a massive gap in the market that only you can fill. If you never start this business, you'll regret it forever."

Naomi was absolutely right: launching *Fidelis* as a Happiness-Centred Business was one of the best things I've ever done professionally. She had always been great at giving me motivational speeches and that one was particularly important. Both of us are still in awe of everything that the team achieved. I remember when I was doing my paper rounds as a lad and *The Financial Times* was the paper that all the business owners would order. I never imagined that my entrepreneurial skills would end up on those world-famous salmon pink pages. Never let anyone tell you that there's such a thing as a 'bad job'. Any job builds key skills. Sometimes that job might require you to cycle round in pouring rain. Other times you might have weeks of shifts scrubbing down cellars. If you put your all into any job you have, you can achieve incredible things. People who get on with things and get things done in a calm and professional manner will always offer huge value to any organisation. I would never have been able to create so much value for others through the *Fidelis* sale without the experience of adding value every day in all those jobs that formed the earlier part of my life.

# Life after the sale...

After selling *Fidelis*, there was a question over what I was going to do next. Tragically, many entrepreneurs suffer from depression after selling their businesses. The purpose that drove every day of their lives, often for more than a decade, has gone and they're not sure what to do with all the time and money that they now have available. For me, keeping my head in the business world was key to making the most of my professional life after *Fidelis*.

No Problem is Permanent

Did walking around in my slippers and watching TV seem appealing? Not a chance! There were still deals to be done, business owners to help and careers to nurture. True to form, the phone rang with life-changing news. This time, Tony was calling me with an amazing offer:

"How would you feel about becoming a partner in our M&A business? Dozens of managed services business owners build great teams which they then struggle to market to potential buyers. As a result, they achieve considerably lower final sale prices than they deserve. *Vexus* is committed to helping these talented entrepreneurs to enjoy absolutely all of the success that they've worked so long and hard for. Your expertise can help them to navigate the many challenges of business sale and achieve optimal conclusions. You can also help them to make cultural and procedural improvements so that their businesses create more value and attract more interest from investors. While you'll be a partner in our Facilities Management division, we both know that you can build businesses that redefine the industry. 'Facilities Management' is the term that's more conventionally used so we would prefer to use that instead of 'Managed Services' in your new role's title."

Helping other entrepreneurs to sell their businesses was a role that hadn't crossed my mind previously, purely because I always insist on doing something myself before offering to advise others on that area. Although *Keen Kleen* was sold to Peter after the restructure, it wasn't sold on terms that I had hoped for. It was a sale made out of necessity rather than a long-planned, strategic exit. The *Fidelis* sale was totally different. The growth of my Happiness-Centred Business allowed me to leave on my own terms. That's what every entrepreneur wants: the ability to choose when to step away from their business and enjoy the rewards of all their hard work.

After achieving this success, I felt sufficiently qualified to advise fellow business owners in my sector on how to do it themselves. So many people throw up a few posts on social media and suddenly think they're qualified to advise on M&A. They're not. Sadly, a number of experienced and successful business owners have fallen for some of these *virtual* executives' claims, only to be let down and lose hundreds of thousands (and sometimes millions) of pounds when things get difficult. A few posts here and there can't achieve breakthroughs in tough negotiations. Negotiations can hit road bumps at any time and only

## Full circle

genuine and hard-earned expertise can help you to navigate them. As people's livelihoods hang in the balance during these negotiations, I strongly believe that all business owners should have access to proper M&A professionals.

That's why my immediate response to Tony was: "That would be amazing, thank you so much. Business owners deserve proper advice when navigating sales processes and I would be honoured to contribute to that as part of your team, which did such fantastic work for me. If you think that having 'Facilities Management' in my role's title will make it easier for those business owners to find us, then that's fine with me. Making 'Managed Services' the go-to term for the cleaning industry is still on my bucket list though."

I would have recommended *Vexus* anyway, so working with them and promoting them officially just made sense. My role with them is not just about facilitating business sale negotiations. It's also about helping business owners to sell at the best possible time. There has been more than one occasion where I've needed to advise against a sale because the company culture in a business is not as good as it could be and is quite literally costing founders hundreds of thousands of pounds (if not more). Sometimes entrepreneurs need months of support to implement processes that will give them not just greater profitability, but the lasting profitability that will allow new owners to inherit debt free, cash generative businesses.

On other occasions, entrepreneurs want to exit their businesses as soon as possible without adapting processes in pursuit of a higher final sale price. In those instances, it's my responsibility to tell these business owners that they won't achieve the final sale price that they were hoping for. While very far from ideal news, many entrepreneurs appreciate hearing this after having some time to mull it over. The news saves them having to spend a fortune consulting loads of different advisers in pursuit of a different answer and allows them the efficient exit they were hoping for in planning the next stage of their lives.

Whenever entrepreneurs feel ready to sell, my biggest challenge is probably in persuading potential buyers to see the true value of the business that they are proposing to acquire. Very often, different deal structures unlock acquisitions that benefit all parties. For example, the final sale price of *Fidelis* included several important bonuses for hitting various EBITDA targets over the following two financial years. EBITDA (Earnings before

## No Problem is Permanent

Interest, Taxes, Depreciation and Amortisation) measures a company's ability to demonstrate real revenue by adding significant costs back onto the company's net profit (profit after tax) to answer the question: how much cash is the company generating before all the bills go out? There are two ways to complete the calculation.

Either you can add Depreciation (losses in value from physical assets like machinery or vehicles) and Amortisation (losses from expiry of non-physical assets like copyrights or patents) back on to your EBIT (often known as operating or pre-tax profit); or you can take your profit after tax and add back on Interest, Taxes, Depreciation, and Amortisation, as well as Director add-backs to show the real value of the business moving on to new ownership. Director add-backs include a director's personal expenses and other non-recurring costs. As they will disappear with the old ownership, new owners won't have to factor them in as costs which could limit their newly acquired venture's profitability.

Whichever way you calculate it, adjusted EBITDA (adjusted to include Director add-backs) is helpful because it gives potential buyers a good idea of how much revenue the company might generate over the coming years. This key piece of data also gives them the option of incentivising the company's existing team to generate certain levels of earnings before the company fully transitions to new ownership.

Buyers can also structure deals so that some money is repaid if targets aren't met. The key point is that they can base their agreements with sellers on impartial measurements of growth statistics. Numbers have never lied and they never will. The toughest part of brokering deals often comes when potential buyers and sellers just don't see the deal in the same way, despite getting on well with each other and sharing the same values. It's then the broker's job to bring the two together and bridge these gaps so that talks can advance.

Part of this work involves being constantly available. I spend most days talking to prospective buyers. Nobody likes to be kept waiting when they have questions or concerns. Quick responses can prevent minor queries from escalating into significant frustrations that can scupper deals.

I remember once asking Tony if that many phone calls were really necessary.

He said, "Never get frustrated during a deal! You're there to bring two parties to an amicable conclusion. If they are frustrated

Full circle

with each other and you allow yourself to get caught up in that, you'll lose the deal - full stop. Sit down with each party and work through any issues that they have. Then, little by little, everyone moves closer to a sale and a fair deal all round."

Eventually, you get used to the calls. The quicker you respond, the quicker things get done. The main job of any broker is to listen and only then offer advice based on their expertise. We're there to solve problems, not to make them.

Establishing trust with all parties is key to overseeing successful negotiations. There are two things that I always do to build this trust quickly from the get-go. Firstly, introducing the sellers *Vexus* is representing to some of my most trusted contacts for legal and ancillary services makes a huge difference. When people see the quality of service that they receive from this trusted network, they are absolutely confident that I have their best interests at heart. Secondly, I prefer to meet in-person as this is a tried and tested way of establishing excellent long-term professional relationships with both buyers and sellers. Of course, I'm available to meet virtually when that's more convenient for others, but there's something about sitting down with someone that an app can't copy.

These meetings give me a genuine understanding of what makes people tick; what their values are; and what they want out of any deal. This goes beyond price and gets to the heart of why prospective buyers want to acquire the business in question and exactly how it will add value to their existing operations. Bridging gaps then becomes much easier because, apart from anything else, they grow to respect me as a broker and understand that I'm not in it for a fast buck.

It's always difficult to know how you're doing in any role, but owners of larger and larger businesses regularly email me asking me to connect them with major investors- so I must be doing something right. Although dealmaking can be immensely challenging, the gratitude that you feel when the ink dries on contracts and all parties have moved forwards together is extraordinary. Being around brilliant people makes brilliant things happen. Without them, you're on your own with some great ideas but without colleagues and partners to develop those ideas into outstanding mergers, acquisitions and lasting businesses. That's why it's always a privilege when an entrepreneur asks me to contribute to the team achieving this milestone of not just their business journey but their life too.

# Giving back...

Another immense source of gratitude comes from my charity work. The tireless efforts that so many people invest into making others' lives easier is truly inspiring. It's easy to sit at home and complain about things. Actually going out there, making a difference, and helping people (often completely voluntarily) is the vital work that so many wonderful people do every day. It is a privilege to support them too. A charity I particularly enjoy supporting is the *Giles' Trust*. Set up by world-famous cricketer Ashley Giles during his wife Stine's battle with brain cancer, the charity has raised more than £1 million to support Birmingham's QEII Hospital (known locally as the QE) to deliver outstanding care to patients enduring the same battle. As I was treated by Professor Cruickshank at the QE, this cause is immensely close to my heart. Their annual ball is always brilliant. Its most recent *Grease* theme gave me an opportunity to relive one of the highlights of my teenage years.

I still remember how long the queues for the cinema were when the film first came out. My mates all agreed that we had to be the first to see it and we waited for hours to get our seats. It was so worth it in the end though. Nobody minded a bunch of lads dancing down the street singing "Ohhh, *Grease* lighting!" afterwards either, which was ideal. It was a much more relaxed time back then...

Back in 2024, as well as giving all guests wonderful opportunities to relive their own personal memories of the film's release and wear some awesome outfits, the *Giles' Trust* event raised an incredible £47,800 for the QE.

I was pleased to buy a number of great items in the auction, including some concert tickets that Holly had wanted for ages. The annual ball is a regular calendar fixture for as many of my family and friends as can make it, and Naomi spends hours every year decorating the room with beautiful flower arrangements. She does whatever it takes to wow attendees with truly special floral displays and often includes rare and exotic flowers in her arrangements. This always goes well over the modest allowance provided by the charity for the flowers, but Naomi never minds. Making others happy makes her happy, so everybody wins.

I am very fortunate to be surrounded by so many inspiring people every day. Perhaps the biggest inspiration in my life is my

# Full circle

youngest son, Oliver. Despite encountering numerous health challenges, Oliver is the happiest human I've ever met. He constantly makes the sun shine a little brighter whenever he's around and reminds everyone about what truly matters in life.

It's so easy to get overly pre-occupied with the daily grind of life. How long do we all spend dwelling on individual messages or emails each day?

Oliver helps me to put everything in perspective and to embrace the positives of any situation I'm facing in life or in business.

Business life becomes very lonely if you lose faith in humanity. Trusting those around you and taking inspiration from them on a daily basis can turn a flood of professional challenges into a few drops in the ocean.

I still meet up with Sue regularly for lunch at *The Moat House* in Acton Trussell which is the same place we first met when Laurence introduced Sue to me all those years ago. We talk about everything that we're doing now, things that happened at *Fidelis*, and have a great time reminiscing over our careers. She asked me something profound recently:

"If there's anything in your career that you could travel back and change, what would it be…?"

# Chapter Twelve

## Life always gives you another turn

"It's not much further, Mr Ansermoz."

That was a huge relief as I could hardly hear myself think; the noise was absolutely deafening. I was walking through Winson Green Prison (HMP Birmingham) with their ex-offender liaison team, on my way to their huge new industrial cleaning training centre. The team had invited me to talk to offenders about career opportunities in managed services at multiple different levels. Some offenders had the potential to become talented cleaning operatives. Others were more suited to sales or admin jobs within the industry. Whatever their interests, my job was to help these people to stay out of prison once they'd been released. More importantly for them, in the short-term, attending my talks would help them to qualify for release on temporary licence (ROTL) and see their families for whole days or even overnight before returning to prison. That being said, I didn't just want to give sessions that they sat through bored rigid after only attending to tick a box. I felt like I owed it to them to deliver real value in each session.

Adding this value was loads tougher than it looked on paper.

The biggest question I had was:

"How can I relate to these people and share my knowledge in a way they'll find useful?"

Like many members of the public, I was more than a bit nervous about walking into a prison, let alone working with offenders. Different media outlets often paint offenders as dangerous individuals who don't have anything constructive to offer society. According to many reports, there are prisoners who should stay there, not offenders deserving a second chance and willing to transform their lives.

In the overwhelming majority of cases, this perception of offenders couldn't be further from the truth and is actually harming the UK's economy. While a number of offenders can never be released from prison, this group only accounts for a small percentage of the UK's total prison population. In England & Wales, less than 10% of a total of nearly 90,000 prisoners are currently serving life sentences. That gives well over 80,000 opportunities to help offenders to build fulfilling, legitimate careers after they leave prison. Giving them these opportunities is in everyone's interest. Society needs them to be making the most of their skills and paying tax on earned income rather than costing taxpayers a fortune by getting locked up again.

On talking to some of the offenders who attended my sessions, I began to realise just how unfortunate many of their situations were. Adding value often starts by listening and these conversations were no exception. Before their convictions, quite a few of the offenders had found themselves in the wrong place at the wrong time and reacted to a provocation in a way that had dozens of unintended consequences, including sending them to prison.

One of the blokes inside told me his story:

"I was walking down the road with my wife, not causing anyone any bother. Then, this horrible little man comes up and starts trying to harass her. We both tell him to stop but he keeps on. Then he looks like he's about to get violent. I do what anyone would do in that situation and defend my wife by pushing this idiot out of the way. He only goes and cracks his head on the nearest garden wall and dies. Then I get done for manslaughter and have wasted most of the last decade of my life in here."

A difference of inches would have saved both that individual's life and that offender's future. There are so many ways that a situation like that could have played out without long-term harm coming to anyone involved. The conflict management skills that business teaches you could have provided the gentleman I was talking to with key tools for diffusing the situation without using his hands. Sometimes people just don't know how to turn their lives in a different direction. They take the steps that they're used to in response to whatever they're facing and, very often, those steps lead them straight to bad places.

There were other situations where offenders had displayed extensive entrepreneurial acumen in the wrong ways. Organising their operations differently or changing their product ranges could have created hugely successful businesses, helping other talented individuals to build meaningful and prosperous long-term careers. Sadly though, they didn't, lives were damaged and they ended up serving years in prison.

One offender told me exactly how he'd created a vast fraud instead of a legitimate (and huge) transportation business:

"You know how you can go to Calais and bring back some alcohol and cigs without paying VAT?"

"If it's for personal use – yes," I said, knowing what was coming next.

"Well, Lloyd, I started doing that and selling the bits I didn't need to my mates. After all, no one can smoke a whole car boot full of cigs on their own. Then I started bringing a bit more back each time, and eventually, I filled a van. After that, the van became a truck, then a few trucks. We were making a fortune. Then the police got wind of it, confiscated everything and I've been stuck here for the last five years, with a few more to go....

And that's if I'm lucky. If I can't get parole, then I might not get out for another decade."

After a short pause, the most useful reply I could offer him was:

"What about if I show you how to handle the paperwork that you would need to build a completely legal transportation business? With your business nous, you could easily do very, very well. You just need to take a different turning when you get to Customs. The hardest bit of any business is finding customers who

Life always gives you another turn

you can build long-term partnerships with. You can do that with your eyes shut. You just need to set it up and run it in the right way. You can pay someone to do the admin, but it needs to get done properly.

"While you're still in here, my sessions will help you to demonstrate that you're learning new skills and explain exactly how you plan to turn your life around. Then, you'll wow the parole board and get back to your family ASAP."

He sat back as if a colossal weight had just vanished from his shoulders. He knew that his life was about to get a whole lot easier in just a few years' time.

He was absolutely elated and shouted, "I'd never thought of fully registering as a transportation company!"

A smile (that had clearly been gone for some time) gradually re-emerged.

"I just did what I knew and kept on with it because it was making money. All of that paperwork just seemed like a massive headache, so I avoided it. It just seemed like a waste of time that I could spend making more money and providing a better life for my family. Now they've lost everything we had, and the kids are too young to understand why."

"That's why having the right people in place in your organisation makes all the difference," I reassured him. "Admin isn't my strongpoint either, which is why I find people who love it and pay them to keep me one step ahead of the regulations. That way, there's never any risk of me even accidentally breaking the rules or filling out forms late and facing fines."

"Right...so with the right team in place, I really can build a successful business and put this nightmare chapter of my life behind me?" he asked in one of the most hopeful voices I've ever heard.

"Yes! Absolutely! I'll start showing you how today-" was all the only thing left for me to say.

He quickly became one of the best and most regular attendees at any of my sessions. Now he runs a hugely successful transportation business and pays significant amounts of VAT, Corporation Tax and Income Tax to HMRC every year.

It was a huge relief that I was able to get on with some of the offenders, and slowly, preparing my sessions became easier and their benefits became more obvious to everyone involved.

Anyone can turn their life around if they are truly committed to changing. They just need the knowledge and tools to do it.

## No Problem is Permanent

Imagine you're walking through a park in the dark. It looks to you like your only option is to follow the path ahead. However, an experienced jogger breezes past you with their new headlamp on and takes a shortcut to the left past some lovely trees. Their experience taught them that the turning was there - you had no idea. Different life experiences can make something that seems obvious to you a fantastic surprise for someone else.

My life could have taken a very different series of turns than it did, on multiple different occasions. There was always something dodgy going on in Chelmsley Wood when I was growing up. From struggling local retailers trying to pull a fast one with their books to regular cases of violent crime, it was very difficult to avoid all that and stay on the straight-and-narrow. Working at the bakery and then taking the risk to travel to Manchester and clean those cellars not only gave me a way out of the area; these experiences also helped me to start building the skills and know-how to succeed professionally.

If I'd decided to get my first experience of work with the lads hanging out down the road, I'd almost certainly be writing a prison diary rather than this book. Crime never pays. You should always use your skills to help others and add value to wider society. Sadly, so many young people nowadays get into things that they don't fully understand, either because they think those things are cool or they just can't stand poverty anymore. Then they get sucked into a whirlwind of negative, damaging and (horrifically) sometimes even life-threatening outcomes.

Thankfully, I had my Granda and my Dad to show me the ropes at the bakery. Quite often though, young people today don't have those positive role models and don't know how to manage all of the challenges that life throws at them. They aren't bad people; they're talented people lacking proper advice and guidance.

Business owners can be those positive role models who help young people to get set up in the world. Helping a young person - or an older person who made mistakes when they were younger - to build a fulfilling life for themselves and their family is the most important thing that anyone can do. If you find that you've got a bit more time on your hands than you used to, then why not get in touch with local schools, youth clubs and prisons to see what you can do to help?

Even if only a few people turn up to hear you speak, changing people's lives makes it all worth it. You don't need a big audience to get your message across effectively. Helping one person to earn

## Life always gives you another turn

legitimate and long-term wealth can transform communities for generations. Giving back is a privilege. There's nothing quite like the happiness you feel when someone you've helped makes the right turn and can put a difficult chapter of their life behind them forever.

Helping others is a blessing that comes from experiencing both the good, the bad, and the truly grotesque moments that life can throw up. Trying to get through everything and succeed without asking for help puts you under an enormous amount of pressure. Nobody needs that. The teachings from Tony Robbins, Deepak Chopra and many others, whose work I have spent many years studying, have blessed me with the ability to cherish life from a truly unique perspective. Without this new outlook, I would have never broadened my business interests from purely making money to helping others along the way as they built fulfilling careers. I also would never have fully appreciated the role of wonderful teams in building not just successful businesses but giving my life more meaning too.

Success comes from the support you receive from others. I wouldn't be sitting in this lovely house typing this book without the inspiration and support of Naomi, Holly and Oliver, Ian and his partner Steph, and our wonderful grandchildren Libby, Kayden and Macey. I have so much to be grateful to them all for and will forever love them for all that they have given to me. They continue to inspire me beyond all belief, and I am so happy to have them in my life.

The teams and partners who my businesses depended on to grow, and the doctors who saved my life several times. Other people, not money, make the world go round. The sooner you truly appreciate that, the sooner you'll achieve your goals.

Back at *The Moat Hose* in Acton Trussell, it took me a while to answer Sue's question about whether there's anything I wish I could change in my career with the support of a time machine. Everything seems to have happened for a reason and even the awful things have taught me loads about life.

After an extended pause, it was obvious that I'd been staring into my cup of tea for too long and needed to say something. The first thing that came to mind was:

"I wish I'd asked for help earlier, but I have no regrets. You can't change the past, but you can definitely change the future."

There's always a way forwards in any situation. I remember when we had that second meeting and you saw how dire a

## No Problem is Permanent

financial state *Keen Kleen* was really in. You showed me and all of us a way out of it. On other occasions Laurence, Carl and so many others were there throughout the journey into *Fidelis* and towards the deal to sell (which was always in our 10-year plan for the business). They saw solutions where others might only have seen obstacles.

Without all of you, I would have never understood the true value of faith in other people. All of us entrepreneurs need self-confidence, but without faith in others, life is just constant pressure. Knowing that everyone in what came together as my *Fidelis* team would always do everything to the highest standard eased the burden on me indescribably. I could focus on the aspects of the business that I was most passionate about, because everything else just ran like clockwork. Appreciating that and trusting my team more, earlier in my career, would have made life so much easier and more enjoyable.

Nowadays, I can enjoy life to the fullest. I only wish I could have felt like that in the 90s and early 2000s."

Sue looked out of the window before replying:

"I learnt loads from everyone too. We all helped each other to get through business, life and create better futures for hundreds of different families. There's never a point of no return in life. Even the toughest challenges are opportunities to rebuild, innovate and come back stronger. With the right team and the right plan, you can achieve anything."

"That couldn't be more true!" I agreed enthusiastically before finishing my tea. "After all, no problem is permanent."

# No Problem is Permanent

# About Lloyd Ansermoz

Lloyd has spent decades helping people to achieve peak performance. Having employed more than 700 people over the course of his career, Lloyd completely understands the vital importance of learning and self-development for personal and professional growth. Changing his own mindset helped him to sell two businesses for £multi-million returns.

Lloyd started out cleaning an industrial bakery and then travelled around the country cleaning factory cellars of hazardous asbestos. From there he progressed to managing and growing key strategic relationships, including a partnership with one of the UK's most important dairies. He then moved into franchising before running cleaning operations across whole regions for a national sector leader. Lloyd also founded two of his own highly successful businesses in the sector. During this time, he was forced to deal with many hurdles in his personal life: including divorce and two battles with cancer.

What got Lloyd through?

It wasn't a desire to earn ever more money for himself. Although that was a major motivator early in his career, Lloyd realised over the years that this selfish approach to business life was holding him back. Faith in people allowed Lloyd's businesses to create cultures that empowered colleagues to be their best selves. Trusting and empowering colleagues helped Lloyd to turn seemingly impossible problems into sources of personal and professional happiness.

He's here to help you overcome any obstacles you're facing and achieve your goals. After all, no problem is permanent.

# Tom O'Brien

Tom O'Brien helps ambitious entrepreneurs to share their knowledge and experience across a whole range of written content. When he's not writing you can normally find him at a lunch or in a think tank. He holds a BA (Hons) degree in French from the University of Liverpool.

# Quotes about the author

Here are a few of the lovely things that colleagues and clients have said about Lloyd:

"Lloyd Ansermoz is one of the most inspirational entrepreneurs that I have ever met."

"Having built and sold not one, but two successful businesses, Lloyd is still generous, humble and down to earth. I would recommend Lloyd without hesitation to anyone seeking a mentor, advisor or NED."

"Having worked with Lloyd for over 17 years, I would recommend him to any ambitious business owner who wishes to accelerate their company growth and achieve the returns they desire."

"Lloyd is an incredible person and mentor."

"Trying to keep this to a small statement about what's great about Lloyd is going to be difficult. I cannot recommend him highly enough."

"Working with Lloyd has been the most fulfilling and enjoyable experience of my career."

# LAMWYK & CO LTD

## About Us

Lamwyk was established in 2012 to promote independent thinking and shared insights under the banner "Reach and Range."

We started with round table discussions for professionals to share insights, knowledge and best practice.

During Covid we moved online and produced a limited run of short videos.

We also launched the quarterly Lamwyk Journal, which is much like a digital publisher's commonplace book.

In 2024 this reached a circulation of over 90,000 professional connections.

In 2025 we began to publish business books to reach an even wider audience.

Printed in Great Britain
by Amazon

47a367f9-6ca5-4f96-be1d-6ee6fc5b0534R03